'Business is a lot like racing. It's about: competition, **speed** & **winning**. There is only one thing missing - **great Pitstops!**

Ray Collis & John O' Gorman

Plus 2,750 managers across 12 industries

www.growthpitstop.com

ISBN: 978-1-907725-04-3

© **Growth Pitstop**

Dublin – Oslo - London

ADVANCE PRAISE

'Most organizations have few alternatives to profitable growth; it's a pre-requisite for maintaining valuations, expanding opportunities and attracting relevant talent, and other core business issues.

In Growth Pitstop, Ray Collis and John Gorman dissect the cross-functional requirements for growth, and their engaging Formula-1 model is more than a metaphor: chapter by chapter, their book provides an actionable agenda that managers can use for accelerating growth in their firms.'

Prof. Frank Cespedes
Harvard Business School
Author of *'Aligning Strategy and Sales'* (HBR Press, 2014)

'Growth Pitstop provides a business model that can prepare companies for the ever increasing speed of business. I've spent my whole life in a fast paced business, where success comes to teams who ask their people to sometimes stretch beyond their best. Growth Pitstop captures the essence of how to do this.

Many people admire the great skills of the world's most successful motorsports teams, and wish that their corporate team could operate at that level. Now they can learn how to do it'.

Derek Daly
F1™ Racer (64 Grand Prix races)
Author of *'Race to Win'* & *'How to Become a Complete Champion Driver'*

CONTENTS

Part 1: The SPEED FACTOR

Part 2: SPEED TESTS

INSPIRATION

Imagine racing legend Michael Schumacher sitting with strategy guru Michael Porter at one table and Harvard professor Frank Cespedes with F1™ luminary Frank Williams at another. Elsewhere in the room author and ex-P&G CEO Alan Lafley is sitting with racing legend Alain Prost and stellar strategy consultant Chris Zook is talking to the Red Bull team's Christian Horner.

Also in the room are Garry Hammel, Patrick Leincioni and Henry Mintzberg. This book imagines the fascinating conversations that would result on topics such as; performance, innovation, teamwork, leadership and talent. Most important of all; the drive to win!

This book reveals how leading figures in the world's fastest sport share the same interests as the CEOs of the world's fastest growing companies and the big names of the world's most prestigious business schools. It brings the principles of winning in the world's most demanding sport to competing in the world's fastest changing markets drawing inspiration from:

- The **passion, discipline and skill** of motor racing champions such as; Michael Schumacher, Niki Lauda, Ayrton Senna and Lewis Hamilton to name just a few.

- The **drive for excellence and innovation** of leaders in the sport such as; Bernie Eccleston, Ron Dennis, Colin Chapman, Frank Williams, Mark Gallagher, Derek Daly and Eddie Jordan.

Thanks for the Inspiration

'You never really know how quick you are before you reach F1™.'

Jean Alesi, Driver[1]

F1™, FORMULA ONE™ and FORMULA 1™ are trademarks of Formula One™ Licensing BV, a Formula One™ group company. They are used in good faith in accordance with 'Nominative Fair Use' to describe the qualities and characteristics of these highly unique and special events / sports / pursuits.

The Growth Pitstop™ is <u>not</u> affiliated with or has <u>not</u> been endorsed or sponsored by Formula One™ in any manner, nor licensed any intellectual property for use in this book.

The Growth Pitstop™, The Sales Strategy PitStop™, Revenue Circuit™ are registered marks of The ASG Group.

Other trademarks referenced, including: Scuderia Ferrari F1™, Lotus F1™, NASCAR™, Goolge™, Mercedes™, Red Bull™ and Nike™ are the registered trademarks of the respective organizations.

Dedicated to Michael Schumacher and his family.

*My philosophy is never to think you have achieved it! Always looking
for the millimeters/seconds ... find it on lap 50 of the third day!*
Michael Schumacher[2]

GRATITUDE

The Growth Pitstop™ is a 9-year project which has spanned 47 countries and 12 industries. It has involved hundreds of workshops – or what we call pitstops - on the topic of growth. These have been attended by managers from organizations, such as; IBM, BT, 3M and Medtronic to name just a few. Although there are simply too many people and even companies to mention, we owe a depth of gratitude to you all.

A special thanks to all those quoted and referenced in this book – their ideas and research have fueled our own work. And finally thank you to those in the pit lanes at tracks from Monte Carlo to Abu Dhabi - your focus, discipline and teamwork inspires a new standard for performance.

From Ray in Oslo:

To my family, Jeanette, Kevin and Andreas, this book is for you with love. To my mother Theresa and departed father Desmond, as well as my brothers Damien and Gavin, special thanks for your encouragement and support. To my Norwegian family and friends, 'tusen takk' for your support.

From John in Dublin:

To my wife Janel and daughter Symone, you both keep me grounded and ensure I stay honest with myself. You are my greatest supporters, despite the sacrifices you both make as I travel around the world. To my parents and my sister Mary, I owe my belief in people, learning and being curious about human behavior to you. Your unending support and words of encouragement continue to inspire my work and research.

SECTION 1

INTRODUCTION

& EXECUTIVE SUMMARY

A bad day at the racetrack beats a good day at the office.
Race Saying

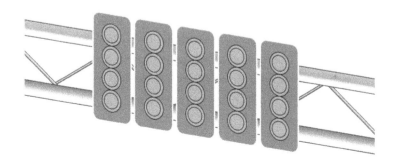

THE ULTIMATE QUESTION

What percentage of your company's full growth potential is presently being exploited? That simple yet powerful question is a great place to start a senior management conversation. Indeed, it is such a powerful question that, of all the possible openings to this book, we wanted to begin with it. So here it is again:

> *Q: What percentage of your company's full growth potential is presently being exploited? Circle the point on the scale below.*

0%   10%   20%   30%   40%   50%   60%   70%   80%   90%   100%
(% of full growth potential exploited)

Unless you marked 100% on the scale, this book was written for you. Across the thousands of managers that we have benchmarked the average response to the 'growth potential' question is 55%. That is a very positive and encouraging figure – it means that most organizations have lots of potential for growth. But it leads us to the next question: *With so much potential to accelerate growth what is stopping you?*

How to accelerate growth? Sustained profitable growth that is. Is the solution to be found in strategy, execution, leadership, innovation or change? Does accelerating your organization or unit's growth depend on; new products, markets, channels or sources of competitive advantage? Well it depends on who you ask or where you look for inspiration!

GOING FASTER: THE NEW EXPERTS

In this book we seek advice on accelerating growth from the 'usual suspects'; business professors and writers (over 400 of them), as well as senior managers (some 2750 of them).   But we also asked another group who is every bit, if not more; obsessed with speed; high speed racers and race team managers. They also talk about; performance, competition and talent, for example, but they come at it from a very different perspective. The language and stories they used to describe the requirements of winning on the racetrack turned out to be a powerful vehicle for communicating the requirements of winning in the marketplace.

Talking about going faster at the same time as growing faster resulted in better conversations, deeper insights and more creative solutions. In short the racing perspective emerged as a powerful metaphor to reframe the cross-functional requirements of business success, as well as a powerful means of communicating the latest research into organizational growth, leadership, change and strategy - execution.

YOU ARE A CHAMPION!

Going fast requires a great driver, but that is hardly a secret. That is you - the corporate equivalent of a champion racer, such as Lewis Hamilton, Nikki Lauda or Michael Schumacher!

Q: *Are you a <u>champion driver</u> when it comes to the performance of your organization, business unit or team?*
Circle the point on the scale

0%	10%	20%	30%	40%	50%	60%	70%	90%	100%

(% confidence that you are a champion driver)

You have the talent, the passion and the skill of a champion racer – don't you? But is that enough to make your organization go/grow faster? What else does a great driver need?

Race Champions such as Michael Schumacher - the most successful F1™ race champion ever - clearly possess great drive, passion and skill. But listen to them talk and you will quickly learn that they attribute their success to more than just their own personal efforts and abilities (considerable though they may be). There are valuable insights here for managers who want to drive their businesses forward. We call them Speed Tests, they reveal the requirements of going faster and they are as relevant in the boardroom as they are on the race track. Let's examine them now.

SPEED TEST 1: **MACHINE**

How fast you can go depends on what you are driving - whether it is a car or a business. That is Speed Test number 1. As the champion driver needs a high performance race machine, the Champion CEO requires a powerful Revenue Generating or Value Creating Machine.

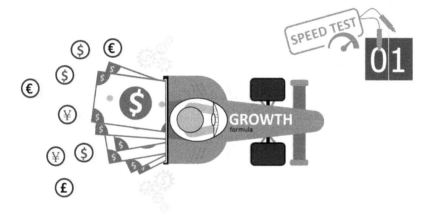

A driver can only go as far and as fast as his or her vehicle will take him or her. For a CEO or senior manager, the organization's business units, divisions and teams are the vehicles of growth. Within each the strategies, structures, systems and process that generate revenue (for the business) and create value (for shareholders, customers and society) are the machinery to accelerate growth. But clearly some vehicles/machines are more powerful than others.

Q: *Is your organization (and its various business units) powered by a high-performance revenue generating / value creating machine?*
Circle the point on the scale below.

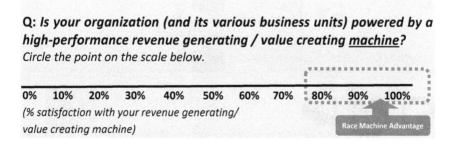

0%   10%   20%   30%   40%   50%   60%   70%   80%   90%   100%
(% satisfaction with your revenue generating/
value creating machine)

Race Machine Advantage

If you rated your revenue generating/value creating machine at 75% or above, then you may have an advantage – a Race Machine Advantage. But if you rated it lower your machine is probably slowing your organization down and Section 5: The Growth Machine is for you.

> It's a never ending battle of making your cars better and also trying to be better yourself.
> Dale Earnhardt[3]

Yet any successful driver will tell you there is no such thing as the perfect machine. It needs to be worked on constantly - set up for the race, optimized during the race and worked on in between races. **Going faster requires great pitstops.** That leads to Speed Test number 2 and it is as relevant to winning in the marketplace as it is to winning on the racetrack.

SPEED TEST 2: **PITSTOP**

For the race machine to perform at its best requires regular mid-race pitstops. So too the Revenue Generating / Value Creating Machine requires ongoing maintenance, optimization and adjustment. But there is no time to waste, pitstops have to be fast.

The pitstop is a metaphor for performance management generally, and an agile approach to strategy and execution in particular. Before setting out on the track the machine needs to be set up for success (gear ratios, choice of tires and so on). This is the equivalent of setting your strategy, including; product-market decisions, sales and marketing activities, resourcing and so on. But optimizing for success is not a once off pre-race event. Rather it takes place at regular intervals throughout the race. The pitstop is the means by which driver and machine can address performance issues and adapt to changing track conditions, the moves of a competitor and so on. This has to happen mid-race because it is too late once the race is over. As a manager you are also in a race - a race to quarter or year end with competitors in fast pursuit. But will you take a pitstop and, if you do; will it enable you to go faster, or just slow you down?

Q: *Does your organization _pitstop_ it's strategies, projects and initiatives in a way that helps it to win?*
Circle the scale below.

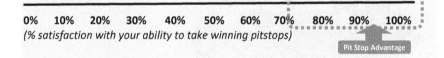

0%   10%   20%   30%   40%   50%   60%   70%   80%   90%   100%
(% satisfaction with your ability to take winning pitstops)

If you rated your management team's ability to speedily and effectively execute, review and adjust projects, strategies and initiatives at 75% or above you may have a Pitstop Advantage. But if you rated it lower then this area is probably slowing your organization down and Section 6: The Pitstop is for you.

The race track is an increasingly popular metaphor to communicate the demands of; accelerating innovation, out-maneuvering competitors and responding swiftly to fast changing markets. But every race track has a pit lane and ironically it is there that managers can see the behaviors and capabilities that are required for effective cross-functional collaboration, business agility and innovation.

Great drivers require great machines and those machines require great pitstops, but what determines the greatness of a pitstop? Well, that is Speed Test number 3; the pit team. Going faster also requires a great pit team.

SPEED TEST 3: **PIT TEAM**

Winning a motor race depends on the ability to quickly pull the car into the pit lane and to perform essential improvements without falling behind. But it has to be fast, in just 2-3 seconds a team of up to 20 will surround the car and in an incredible display of teamwork do what is required to optimize the car and send it on its way. The same needs to happen when a cross-functional senior management team comes together to plan and review key growth strategies, projects and initiatives.

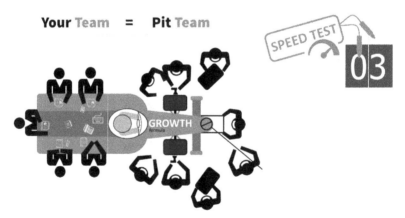

The machinery of business is only as powerful as the pit team that maintains and supports it. Similarly, the growth performance and potential of your organization depends on your managers working effectively as a pit team. The highly choreographed precision of the pit team sets the new standard for teamwork and cross-functional collaboration. It exemplifies; urgency, discipline, trust and a passion for winning. While each person on the pit team has their own role and responsibilities, they are interdependent rather than independent and all share the same goal; making the car / organization go faster.

A pit team is any team that works together effectively to maximize the chances of winning. But when it comes to growth the ultimate pit team is the cross-functional senior management team. Of all the teams in the organization it is the performance of this team that matters most.

Q: How well do your senior managers work together as a Pit Team?
Circle the point on the scale below.

| 0% | 10% | 20% | 30% | 40% | 50% | 60% | 70% | 80% | 90% | 100% |

(% satisfaction with how managers work as a pit team)

Pit Team Advantage

It takes a team to win a race, even if there is only one person on the stand collecting the trophy. The ability of senior cross-functional managers to work like a pit crew is perhaps the ultimate competitive advantage. If you rated your cross functional team at 75% or above in terms of its ability to work effectively together, then you probably have an advantage in this area – a Pit Team Advantage. But if the score was lower this area is probably slowing your organization down and Section 7: The Pit Team is for you.

A quick recap: A great driver requires a great machine, which in turn requires great pitstops and an effective pit team. However, the environment in which these come together is another important determinant of success. That is Speed Test 4: the pit lane.

> *Never think that success is down to your own performance alone. If you start listening only to yourself you take the first step back towards the bottom. The flowers of victory belong in many vases.*
> Michael Schumacher[4]

SPEED TEST 4: **PIT LANE**

The pit lane is where it all comes together - the driver, car, pitstop and pit team. The corporate pit lane is the environment in which teams work, and most importantly; win together. It is not just the physical space, but also the social, cultural and psychological context.

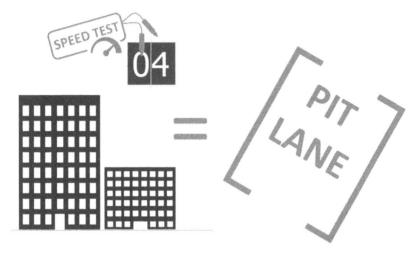

The race pit lane is a high pressure environment with lots of noise, heat and of course; fast moving vehicles. The same can apply in organizations where personalities, politics and competing priorities distract from an open and honest dialog regarding performance and potential. All this results in the risk of a wheel coming off the car as it accelerates out of the pit lane – evident in the form of problems around implementation or execution in respect of business projects or strategies.

Q: Does your organization's environment facilitate effective cross functional collaboration, innovation and change?
Circle the scale below.

| 0% | 10% | 20% | 30% | 40% | 50% | 60% | 70% | 80% | 90% | 100% |

(% satisfaction with your organization's winning environment)

Pit Lane Advantage

A winning environment – one that facilitates effective cross-functional collaboration, learning and innovation - is Speed Test number four. The culture of the organization often sets it maximum speed. If you rated this low, then Section 8: The Pit Lane is for you. Be warned however it is the so called 'soft stuff' that so often proves the hardest to manage.

Is this the ultimate source of competitive advantage?

Like the discovery of a new species in the animal kingdom, business writers and university academics are pointing to the existence of a new source of competitive advantage in business and industry. There are even claims that this newly discovered advantage represents the origin of the species - the ultimate source of competitive advantage or the foundation upon which all other advantages - from R&D to marketing - are built. Yet despite its emergence as one of the hot topics in management today, it won't come as any great surprise to most experienced managers. They know or at least suspected that it has a key role to play in corporate success and moreover they also know that it is a scarce commodity in many organizations. The new source of competitive advantage is cross-functional collaboration among senior management in respect of the key growth priorities of the organization. In particular research suggests that the ability of a management team to come together regularly to openly and effectively dialog the priorities and performance of the organization is a real indicator of the growth potential of an organization. Some call it the ability to have 'a strategic conversation', we call it the ability to pitstop.

> For at least twenty years, people have been studying and writing about the increasing speed of business and the need for organizations to be quicker and much more agile
> John P. Kotter[5]

A SHARED DEFINITION OF WINNING

As the four Speed Tests reveal winning on the race track and winning in the marketplace have a lot in common. They represent the common points of agreement as to the requirements of winning seen from two different but entirely complementary perspectives; the business professor and the champion race driver.

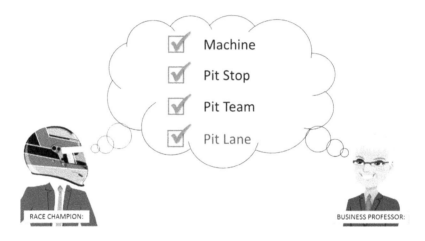

The lesson for managers is: working on the race car (your revenue generating / value creating machine and the strategies, systems and structures that accelerate it) will only get you so far. About 60% of the way according to managers who have participated in Growth Pitstop™ workshops. To reach top speeds managers must work on the pit team too (especially the cross functional senior management team) – that accounts for about 40% of acceleration say managers. This is consistent with the very latest business thinking and industry research which points to the primary importance of organizational health in driving performance.

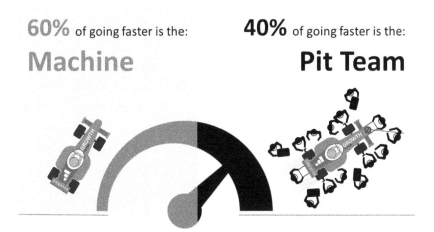

60% of going faster is the: **Machine**

40% of going faster is the: **Pit Team**

Of course it is not a question of whether managers should work on the race machine or the pit team. They need to work on both and to do so in tandem. The means of doing this is the pitstop – that is the ultimate Speed Test. It is the secret of F1™ levels of performance in business.

> Is the performance of your organization or business unit under pressure from more demanding customers, increased competition, new technology or new regulations? Then take a pitstop! The secret to winning in business as on the racetrack - it is effective pitstops.

> *Schumacher drew upon his multiple on - and off-track skills to build the type of environment he needed to win. He never criticized Ferrari, even when the car did not match his obvious skills. He always helped and supported the team and always wore a smile even if he was not on the podium. His classy behavior built an almost unshakable foundation of critical trust and belief within the team.*
> Derek Daly[6]

BE THE F1™ OF YOUR INDUSTRY

Most companies are capable of a few fast laps, but reaching F1™ levels of performance requires accelerating sustained and profitable growth lap after lap and race after race. That is a real challenge even at a modest rate of 5.5% in terms of the top line, bottom line and Return on Assets (ROA)[7]. As the qualification criterion for F1™ status in your industry it means that only a minority of companies can qualify.

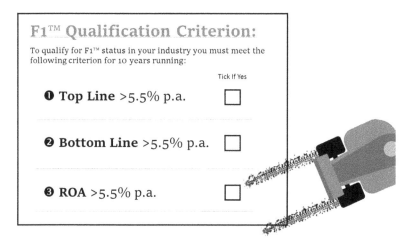

F1™ Qualification Criterion:

To qualify for F1™ status in your industry you must meet the following criterion for 10 years running:

Tick If Yes

❶ **Top Line** >5.5% p.a.   ☐

❷ **Bottom Line** >5.5% p.a.   ☐

❸ **ROA** >5.5% p.a.   ☐

F1™ is an elite club of the super-fast, super agile and super innovative in racing. But who are the high performers – the F1™ - in your industry and are you among them?

Q: *Do you want to be among your industry's highest performers – leading the way in terms of passion, innovation and of course in terms of sustained and profitable growth? That is to be in the F1™ of your industry?*

Reaching F1™ levels of organizational speed and agility requires more and better pitstops. With each pitstop the car and the team gets better.

A Metaphor for Growth

Fast cars, millionaire lifestyles and flowing champaign are all part of F1™. But although these things are inherently appealing they are a relatively superficial view of a sport and business that can inspire in so many ways. F1™ is a high performance culture that is characterized by a passion for winning, as well as levels of speed, agility and passion rarely found elsewhere. It is also a model in terms of skills, teamwork and innovation, as well as its obsession with performance and relentless quest for improvement. These characteristics are key to winning in the boardroom, just as they are on the racetrack. In particular, they represent the basis for competitive advantage in a business environment that is increasingly fast-paced, complex and competitive.

IT IS COMPLEX!

This book adopts an innovative approach, including the use of metaphor, models and cognitive re-framing, to make it easier to access and engage with a topic that is complex and wide ranging. It is a proven approach to engage emerging leaders from Generations X, Y and Z. What it cannot do however is make the challenges of growth any easier. The contents of this book are utterly challenging, as well as tremendously rewarding. But there is no silver bullet here. The pitstop approach requires engaging with the full complexity of growth and adopting a systems perspective that looks beyond people and events to the underlying causes of business success. It also requires combining the hard (strategies, systems and process) with the soft (culture, people and commitment) as well as clever strategy with excellent execution. The focus is not just on short term revenue growth but sustained profitable growth into the longer term and that requires growth in people, innovation, value creation and so on. It is about a situation where all stakeholders can win - shareholders, customers and staff.

Life is all about challenges - and, most important of all, it's about challenging yourself.
Jenson Button[8]

The solution to the challenges of growth won't be found in any one business discipline (e.g. leadership, change, or strategy). Nor will it be found in any one function (e.g. marketing and sales, or finance). A multi-disciplinary and multi-functional approach is required, across multiple time horizons; short term, medium term and long term. The complexity of the material in this book is a reflection of the challenge of growth, in particular sustaining profitable growth in the long term. The meta-model at the core of this book is built upon a complex algorithm and 248 mathematical variables that are highly predictive of growth performance and potential. The benchmarking data presented in the various chapters is based on a sample of 2750 managers and over 320,000 pieces of performance data gathered across 12 industries:

- IT software, hardware and cloud computing
- Banking and Financial Services
- Telecommunications
- Professional Services
- Medical Devices
- Chemicals & Pharmaceuticals
- Retail
- Food & Catering
- Distribution & Transport
- Education & Training
- Non-Profit
- Government & Public Sector

The research behind the Growth Pitstop™ also includes over 600 academic and other references cited in this series of books, in particular the output of the leading consulting houses (McKinsey, Accenture, BCG, Deloitte and PWC) and leading academic institutions (Harvard, Stanford, Columbia and so on). It also integrates the latest in the areas of predictive growth analytics and growth psychology (see Appendix).

DATA-DRIVEN GROWTH

F1™ has been a pioneer in the areas of Big Data, as well as 'the internet of things'. Masses of data are generated from every part of the car while it is running. This data is analyzed at arrays of monitors to determine how the car can go faster. This is vital information for the pit team and is used to guide decisions about the timing of the pitstop, the selection of tires, as well as any other adjustments to be made. Relying on gut instinct won't do.

A pitstop is based on a lot of analysis and data

Analytics enormous amounts of data

This book is based on extensive benchmarking data on every aspect of growth performance. The challenge for managers is to ensure that they have the same level of real time information and analysis to guide their decisions. That is the type of analysis that will enable them to identify opportunities to accelerate growth. To maximize the effectiveness of their pitstops managers can complete the Growth Pitstop™'s PGA (predictive growth analytics) online assessment measuring 248 performance related variables. This can create an index score for any organization (see Predictive Growth Analytics in the Appendix).

WHAT ELSE IS THERE?

The research behind the Growth Pitstop™ is too extensive to fit into just one book. Rather it is presented in a series of 4 books.

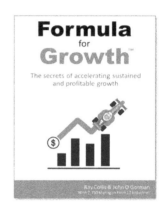

There is more detail on each of the books in the pitstop series in the Appendix. In addition to the series of books the Growth Pitstop™ encompasses a range of workshop tools which organizations can use to run their own pitstops, as well as online growth assessment/analytics – more details in Appendix. But let's get started exploring the requirements of speed.

Part 1:
THE SPEED FACTOR

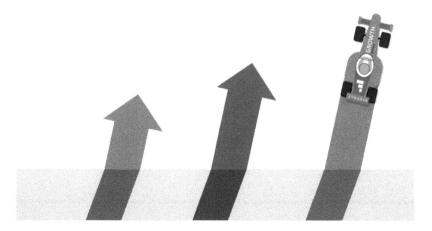

Section 2

THE NEED FOR SPEED

'In the end overtaking is only possible when a faster driver is behind a slower driver. If it is the opposite, then overtaking is not possible'.

Herman Tilke[9]

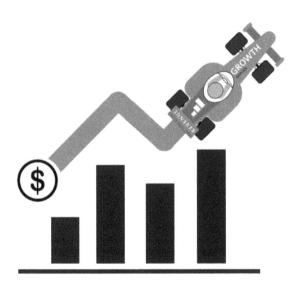

INTRODUCTION

In F1™ winning is about how fast you can go. In business it's about how fast you can grow. Yet research suggests that most organizations never reach their top speed. In this section we will examine why accelerating sustained and profitable growth is the number 1 challenge facing today's CEOs. It is a challenge that many will fail.

Here we will explore the need for speed and begin our quest to reveal the secrets of those high-performing organizations that can accelerate lap after lap to deliver growth that is both sustained and profitable. That is those organizations who demonstrate F1™- like levels of speed, agility and innovation.

GOING FASTER = GROWING FASTER

How do you measure the success of a leader, a management team, a strategy, or for that matter an organization? Well, growth of course. That is sustained and profitable growth, or growth at the top line, as well as the bottom line.

While it may be less glamourous than multi-billion dollar mergers and acquisitions, sustained and profitable growth tends to be largely organic in nature. That is good old fashioned growth - deriving from the ability to acquire, retain and grow customers.

> *While the mergers and acquisition (M&A) route to growth has, at times, been favored by some organizations... growth driven by new market expansion and high-impact innovation has consistently achieved more sustainable success, and is thus becoming a core capability for many companies.*
> Tim Jones, Dave McCormick & Caroline Dewing[10]

Obviously accelerating growth means growing revenue, as well as profits. But focusing on revenue growth alone is not enough. It also requires growth in terms of; customer loyalty, brand reputation, product and marketing innovation, as well as the commitment and skill of the organization's people.

> *Sales by itself is a trailing and often misleading indicator of enterprise performance and value.*
> Frank V. Cespedes[11]

Sustained profitable growth typically requires accelerating performance right across the organisation. That includes; speed of response, speed to market, speed to innovate, speed of decision making and most important of all speed of execution. It also means accelerating; change and innovation, skills and capabilities, strategy and execution, plus a lot more besides.

You Need to *Accelerate:*

- Performance
- Strategy
- Change
- Innovation
- Value Creation
- People & Passion

As well as *GROWTH!*

While defining growth is relatively straight-forward, achieving it is not. That leaves many managers with an unmet need for speed.

> *Grow or die! Every businessperson must understand this stark reality. In today's intensely competitive, technology-driven global marketplace, no enterprise—including yours—can be sustained without growth.*
> Robert Bloom & Dave Conti[12]

MORE SPEED PLEASE!

Do you feel the need for speed in your organization? If you are like most managers the answer is 'YES'. That means you want your organization to go (and indeed grow) faster.

Q: How satisfied are you that your organization is
moving ahead at the right speed?

| 0% | 10% | 20% | 30% | 40% | 50% | 60% | 70% | 90% | 100% |

(% satisfaction with speed of your organization)

Managers rate 'the speed at which their organization is moving ahead' at just 59%. That is the result across the 2,750 of managers who have completed the online Growth Pitstop™ assessment. You could interpret this another way: most managers see their organizations as driving at just 59 mph in a 100 mph zone. Those are certainly far of F1™ speeds!

> In the highly competitive environment of modern business, a common mantra is "grow fast or die quickly", and while that may sound dramatic, it is something that every business professional should remember and revisit.
> Sean Ellis & Morgan Brown[13]

This is not a bad news story however. It shows that most managers see a lot of potential for growth and that is encouraging indeed. They want their organization to go / grow faster. Accelerating growth isn't easy however, especially if that growth is to be sustained and profitable over time.

Those who talk about slowing the pace of growth are really saying that they have had enough, and they should get out before they do the business (their most valuable asset) serious damage.
Rupert Merson[14]

More Speed - Less Inertia?

Our research across 47 markets and 12 industries shows that most managers think their organizations (and their CEO's) are not going fast enough. But such a finding goes against the traditional view of people being slow to change.

There are countless articles and papers written about inertia and resistance to change, yet our data points to an internal 'need for speed' in most organizations. In reality it should come as no surprise that people want to belong to an organization or team that they feel is moving ahead, innovating and making progress. Maybe therefore it is time to challenge the stereotype of the visionary and impatient CEO battling for progress and transformation in the face of internal lethargy and resistance.

Why do our organizations seem less adaptable, less innovative, less spirited, and less noble than the people who work within them?

Garry Hammel[15]

EXPLORING YOUR NEED FOR SPEED

Statistics on the topic of growth make for interesting reading. But they can be a little bit abstract or dry. So before we look at any more data on the subject, let's explore the issue of growth on a more personal level.

Let's apply some creative thinking to the  growth performance and potential of your organization by following these 3 steps:

Step 1: On the page overleaf circle the vehicle that best represents your organization, business unit or team. Indeed, you might like to pick a vehicle for each (if they are different).

You can think of it as a representation of your organization as a revenue generating or value creating machine. Maybe its output is measured in terms of; units produced, volume sold, profit made, shareholder value, or brand image /awareness. It could also be measured in the number of subscribers, supporters, customers or clients, and committed employees or channel partners.

Step 2: Write down the first 3 words that come to your mind to describe the vehicle that you have chosen:

    1. _____

    2. _____

    3. _____

Step 3: Circle the vehicle that best represents your leading competitor(s). Again write down the keywords (as you did in Step 2):

    1. _____

    2. _____

    3. _____

Circle the vehicle that best represents your organization

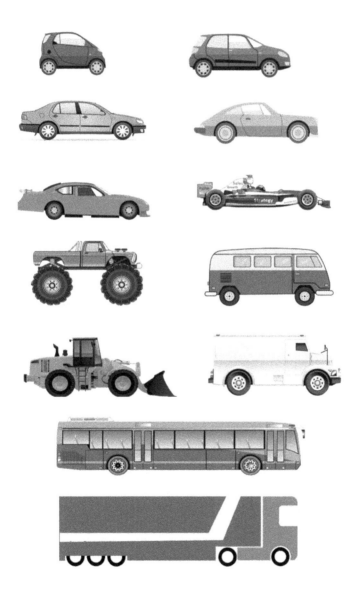

These 3 steps are a creative way of exploring what you see as your organization's need for speed. It is called a projective technique[16]. Although the approach may seem strange, it is actually a sophisticated and powerful way of exploring attitudes, expectations and emotions regarding growth performance and potential. It is also a test of a manager's ability to concisely describe the reality of their organization's growth performance and potential, as well as to 'think outside the box'.

> *...companies will simply lack the ability to find the full potential of growth opportunities if they only focus on quantitative models.*
> Roger Martin[17]

WANT TO GO FASTER?

Now that you have completed the 3 steps, reflect upon the following questions regarding the vehicle that you chose to represent your organization, business unit or team:

- How **fast** is the vehicle that you have chosen? Can it deliver the rate of growth that your organization needs?

- How well does it **handle**? Is it able to out-manoeuvre and overtake the competition?

- Does it have the **power and reliability** required to ensure success?

- Does it have the **driver** to push it to the limit, as well as the **pit team** to keep it on the road?

- Will the car enable your organization to compete and win lap after lap and **year after year**?

Oh and there is one more important question:

- **What is required in order to enable the car to go i.e. grow faster?**

_____

_____

_____

_____

This last question is the most important question of all. It is the question that this book is aimed at answering. After all this book is about how to prime your organization for accelerated growth. All these questions are a test of a management team's ability to get to the core of the issue of growth performance and potential.

Fast Car or Station Wagon? What It Reveals About You

'We are not Formula One™ exclaimed one manager. We are more like a Volvo station wagon - heck some parts of the business are like an old clapped out Volkswagen!'

There it was - in little less than one minute that manager had revealed more than the company's annual report or a presentation to the board of directors. It is a real life example of the power of a metaphor to get at what people are really thinking. The manager's 'clapped-out Volkswagen' remarks were a revelation not just about the company - but the manager too. More specifically it revealed the manager's mind-set - his confidence expectations and attitudes.

What happens next would reveal a whole lot more. In particular, how would those who had heard the remarks respond? For example; would they laugh, nod in agreement, refute the manager's view or seek to better understand it? That would reveal a lot about the mind-set of the group, as well as the culture and health of the team. Would the manager's remarks result in a dialog, an argument, or worse still; silence? Either way what happens next would reveal so much about the growth potential of the organization and its team. Unfolding in the room was the most vital of conversations. Imagine you were there: What would you have said, or done?

GOT A HIGH-SPEED RACER?

When it comes to the racetrack that is your industry or marketplace there are vehicles of every class. Although many are capable of reaching high speeds, most don't have the speed and agility to win consistently over the longer term. Indeed, only about one in ten have Formula One™ levels of acceleration, agility and endurance. That is according to research by consulting giant Bain & Company[18].

Most organizations are capable of completing a number of fast laps. But, spurts of accelerated top line growth are not enough. Sustained profitable growth is the measure of success. That requires what we call triple acceleration.

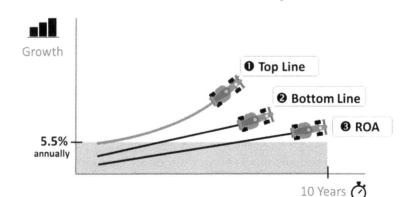

Triple acceleration

For the decade of 1990–2000, only 13 percent of companies achieved all three criteria: a relatively modest rate of growth (5.5 percent in real terms) in (1) sales and (2) operating income, while also (3) earning their cost of capital... and for 2001– 2010, it was only 9 percent— fewer than one in ten companies.
Chris Zook and James Allen[19]

WHAT ARE YOU DRIVING?

This book with its talk of F1™ levels of acceleration and performance – is all about the 5.5% challenge. That is the requirement of accelerating not just the top line but the bottom line and doing it lap after lap for a decade. Think of the triple acceleration as the F1™ qualification criterion for industry performance – shown overleaf. It is the ultimate test.

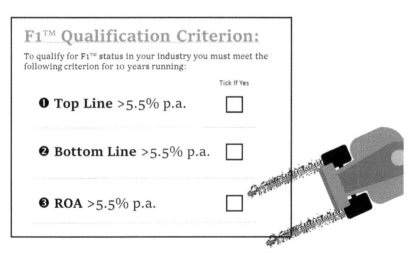

F1™ Qualification Criterion:
To qualify for F1™ status in your industry you must meet the following criterion for 10 years running:

Tick If Yes

❶ Top Line >5.5% p.a. ☐

❷ Bottom Line >5.5% p.a. ☐

❸ ROA >5.5% p.a. ☐

It is a relatively modest rate of growth - 5.5%. For example, in terms of Return on Assets or ROI the result of such compounded rate of growth over a 10-year period would be a 170% return on investment. Although this is not a meteoric ROI, it is out of the reach of most organizations. Yet, it is a challenge to sustain even such a modest 5.5% annually over a decade.

...organizational success has never been more fragile.
Garry Hammel[20]

Triple acceleration is about the ability of the business to create and capture value for all the stakeholders, including customers, staff and last but not least shareholders. It requires blending the short term into the longer term so as to maximize business value and returns. It is a challenge that involves a much richer and deeper meaning of growth – one that looks beyond the sales or the marketing function to engage all stakeholders. It is about accelerating sustained value creation[21].

> *Sustained and profitable growth is rare and becoming increasingly so.*
> Thomas Baumgartner, Homayoun Hatami, et al.[22]

The Exclusive Club of Speed

Companies capable of accelerating sustained profitable growth are the exception, rather than the norm. They are the equivalent of F1™ racers in their industry - capable of accelerating growth in new products and new markets and agile enough to cope with fast changing customers, technologies, channels, regulations and so on. But F1™ is an exclusive club and most companies cannot stay the course when it comes to accelerating and sustaining growth over the longer term. The norm is short spurs of growth, especially at the top line. Long term profitable and sustained growth is the exception, rather than the norm.

> *In aggregate the return on assets of US firms has fallen to one-quarter of its 1965 levels (from 4.1% to 0.9% in 2012).*
> Deloitte[23]

DIFFERENT CARS IN DIFFERENT RACES

In exploring the issue of growth some managers see their overall organization as 'the car'. However, most organisations are in effect running a number of different cars in different races. That means different cars for particular business units, strategies, projects or teams – hopefully all aimed at winning. This is a long standing concept in the area of business strategy. Indeed, many of the most popular tools in strategy owe their origin to it. That includes the poplar BCG's cash cows, stars and dogs, as well as Ansoff's Matrix of market attractiveness and amenability[24].

Portfolio Speed: Different Vehicles in Different Races

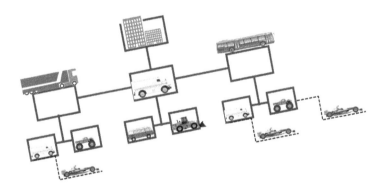

Strategists have long viewed the performance of an organization as resting on how it manages its portfolio of business units, right down to the level of its different products aimed at different markets or segments. The view is that 'a one size fits all' approach does not work when it comes to strategy.

> *'Going beyond averages to adopt a granular perspective on the markets is essential for any company as it shifts its portfolio in search of strong growth...'*
> Patrick Viguerie, Sven Smit & Mehrdad Baghai[25]

Markets are different, so too are the opportunities and challenges they present. Similarly, each business unit or function has its own particular strengths and weaknesses. Thus strategic planning has to be granular if it is to be meaningful – it must take place at business unit level, or team. The strategy needs to be tailored by business line, and market space and geography. These then feed into the overall strategy at a corporate level.

> 'Corporate-level strategy is the vehicle for allocating resources among all of the business units. But it should not be simply the sum of those parts.
> Larry Bossidy, Ram Charan & Charles Burck[26]

We are not suggesting that every organization can or should have the qualities of a F1™ racer. For your core business the metaphor may be a juggernaut, or a big ship - where the emphasis is on maintaining a steady course. But for new markets products and strategies, where being able to pull away from the starting grid fast, execute quick manoeuvres and complete some initial quick lap matters - F1™ is the ideal metaphor. The challenge is therefore to maintain a steady course at the core, while accelerating at the edges.

> ...dynamic capabilities are at the heart of the ability of a business to be ambidextrous—to compete simultaneously in both mature and emerging markets--to explore and exploit.
> Charles O'Reilly & Michael Tushman[27]

You may not be able to accelerate your entire organization in the style of F1™. That might not even be desirable in respect of your core business with its long established modes of doing business and mature processes, its long term strategies, entrenched market position, or captive customers and channels. However, every organization has strategies, capabilities and products or market segments that require a more accelerated approach. In reality your organization needs to have a number of cars in different races.

*About half (55%) of change initiatives meet their initial
objectives, but only 1 out of 4 companies sustain those gains
over the long term.*
Towers Watson Inc.[28]

The need for speed is nothing new. It has long been a concern of
management writers and the metaphors of steering a big ship,
or teaching an elephant to dance have been widely popularized. The
only problem is that elephants and ships are not very fast, or very
agile. That is part of the reason why we have embraced the F1™
metaphor (see Section 3: Metaphor for Growth).

> *Organizations are like elephants-slow to change... Trainers
> shackle young elephants with heavy chains to deeply embedded
> stakes. As time passes, the elephant learns to stay in its place
> and change does not occur.*
> James A. Belasco[29]

WHAT'S YOUR POSITION?

The first step on any strategic journey beings by defining the point of
departure. That is what the Starting Grid exercise is about. It is a high
level situational analysis that asks the question 'where are you now?'.
Just as in racing how far and how fast you can go or grow depends on
what you are driving and where it is on the starting grid. In this way
great growth strategies begin with an honest assessment of
performance and potential.

> *In business most deep strategic changes are brought about by a
> change in diagnosis - a change in the definition of a company's
> situation.*
> Richard P. Rumelt[30]

It is simply not enough to set out where the organization wants to be (the point of arrival) – an aspirational vision or mission statement – unless it is grounded in clear realism regarding the point of departure, as well as a practical step-by step plan to get there. This makes the 'What's Your Position?' exercise a particularly important one.

In every Growth Pitstop™ workshop we ask managers to put their organization or business unit on a starting grid (shown below). Along the top and bottom of the grid you will see that there are numbers ranging from 0% to 100%. These numbers represent your percentage confidence or satisfaction in terms of your organization's or team's growth strategy and performance. So what is your position on the grid?

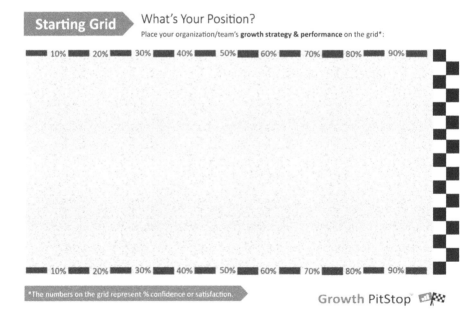

In any discussion about performance and potential it is vital to engage multiple perspectives. This often results in surprises. In a recent Growth Pitstop™ the CEO of a global manufacturer of specialized building materials put the organization at 80% on the grid as did his head of Operations, Marketing and HR. All his national managers put their car/organization at 30% and 50% as below. What a powerful (albeit at times tense) conversation that resulted.

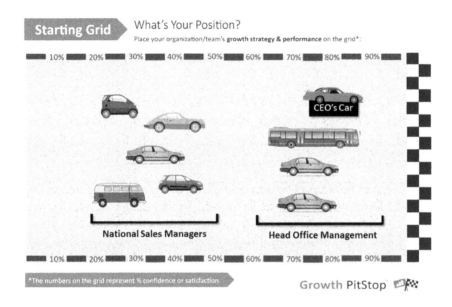

The CEO emphasised that the organization had undergone a major transformation in the previous 16-18 months, including; internal restructuring, the introduction of some new products and removal of some old ones, as well as; a re-alignment of its channels. Acknowledging that these changes entailed a lot of difficult decisions and had been tough on everybody involved, he argued that they left the company in 'a much better position to race forward'. The national managers listened, somewhat surprised at the emotion in the CEO's voice. They conceded that progress had indeed been made, but emphasised that the company had to rebuild its reputation in the marketplace. After a period of being internally focused – it had to once again focus on its relationship with its key customer and channel partners. It was in their words; 'time to build again'.

> *Yet management, in its haste to grow, often overlooks such critical developmental questions as, Where has our organization been? Where is it now? and What do the answers to these questions mean for where it is going? Instead, management fixes its gaze outward on the environment and toward the future, as if more precise market projections will provide the organization with a new identity.*
> Larry E. Greiner[31]

An exercise like this is a test of a management team's ability to openly and honestly discuss performance, as well as potential. It is also a test of your team's creative problem solving abilities and the type of approach to strategy that is increasingly being promoted by experts:

> *The default problem-solving model has its roots in what can be called instrumental rationalism.   ...the belief that business problems can be solved through objective and scientific analysis and that evidence and facts should prevail over opinions and preferences.*
> Christian Madsbjerg & Mikkel B. Rasmussen[32]

In the appendix you will find details of how you can get the starting grid and other materials to run your own Growth Pitstop™.

How Fast Can You Grow?

In F1™ it is all about how fast the car can go – measured in lap times and miles per hour (MPH). In business it is about how fast the organization, business unit or team can grow – measured in revenues, profits, competencies and / or skills. Moreover, it is about the ability of the driver, the pit crew and the larger race team to perform to the limit. But in the meantime consider this: *Have you the right vehicle (revenue generating/value creating machine) in the right race?*

HOW FAST IS FAST?

How fast can your company grow? Well, maybe faster than you think. Especially when you see just how fast others can accelerate. Take those who feature in the Deloitte Technology Fast 500™ for example, where a turbo-charged annual growth rate of 850% is the norm. Yes it is not a typo these companies grew sales 8.5 times each year for at least 3 years. Now that is fast, but it is just the average. At the top of the 2015 list you will find a New York based company called 'Startapp' - it grew by a staggering 21,984% per annum for the period[33]. When you read those growth statistics doubling or tripling growth over a three year period doesn't really seem that scary after all.

Accelerating Growth and Prosperity

The fastest growing companies are variously estimated to account for between 1% and 5% of all companies. Yet research suggests they can account for up to 75% of all newly created jobs[34]. That makes them vital to economic prosperity[35].

> *Because fast-growing young firms account for a disproportionate share of net job creation, policymakers who are worriedly poring over unemployment projections might instead seek to foster the creation of more high-growth firms.*
>
> Robert E. Litan[36]

A F1™ racing car and its driver have a single purpose - that is to accelerate with maximum possible speed around any given racetrack. Indeed it all boils down to this - either you are faster than the competition or you are not. Drivers in F1™ are ultimately measured on one thing and one thing only - that is speed. That is how their cars and the teams who support them are measured too. Does the same apply for managers in your organization?

The Starting Grid

Managers put their cars on the grid. It is a simple yet powerful exercise aimed at quickly revealing how people feel about the performance of their business unit, as well as its potential.

ACCELERATING AT THE CORE, OR EDGES?

Just what will you accelerate and by how much? That is a key strategic question for any business leader. A central issue is what parts of the business are capable of delivering the fastest growth.

Q: Where will your organization's growth come from?

There is a debate among strategist and academics as to where managers should look for accelerated growth. For some companies their core business may not be capable of generating accelerated growth. They may involve mature products and markets where the strategy is one of harvesting revenue from existing customers and channels. Even if the growth potential was there the structured and hierarchal way of managing these mature businesses would likely put the brakes on growth. The speed of many parts of the organization may be bound by slow moving corporate strategies and structures. However that does not mean that the organization cannot accelerate 'around the edges'.

Q: What specific business units, projects or strategies will you accelerate?

> *...the odds of success can be influenced through a more systematic approach to making growth investments, as a portfolio of bets, and to the decoding of lessons from past experiences in terms of what worked.*
> Chris Zook[37]

It is often argued that you cannot accelerate big corporations and that the real opportunities for acceleration are to be found in the creation of new secondary vehicles for accelerated growth at the edges of the organization[38]. However, that does not mean that those fast racers should be unrelated to the core, or have the potential to enhance the core if successful[39]. Once these prove to be successful they can then be progressively integrated more closely to the core of the organization (if that is appropriate). This is an approach that is particularly suited to areas of accelerated change and high levels of uncertainty – areas where greater agility and innovation is required. Specifically, new products, new markets/segments, new channels, new business models. In this way an organization seeks to develop a balanced portfolio of potential growth opportunities – balanced in terms of 'sure things', high risk 'toe in the water' experiments in innovation, market tests to identify longer term potential, quick wins with fast returns and longer term or more speculative investments. The ability to run these experimental fast laps is an important organizational capability. It is the essence of organizational agility.

Luckily, leaders have a viable alternative to prediction: running a portfolio of strategic experiments managed with an eye on the twin imperatives of speed and economy.

Martin Reeves, Knut Haanaes & Janmejaya Sinha[40]

Accelerating Winners

F1™ is used as a metaphor for accelerating innovation, for recapturing agility and for a highly adaptive approach to strategy which is particularly suited to discontinuous change, such as the development of new products, entering new markets, or coping with accelerated change. It is about the ability to take growth related opportunities, projects and priorities and to get them on the track[41]. Then to accelerate some, to pull others off the circuit depending on whether they can prove themselves by means of fast laps. All the time learning what will work and what won't and progressively getting better at identifying and backing winners.

The innovator's dilemma - how executives can simultaneously do what is right for the near-term health of their established businesses, while focusing adequate resources on the disruptive technologies that ultimately could lead to their downfall.
Clayton Christensen[42]

ACCELERATING OPPORTUNITIES

Nowhere is the need for speed greater than in respect of new products and markets. Indeed, the race car is a metaphor for the type of approach that is required to identify the winners of tomorrow[43]. It recognises that great business plans and detailed market analysis alone cannot predict success or failure with anything near the same level of confidence or accuracy as exposure to the market place. Fast-changing markets require giving particular opportunities a race for their money, giving them a few laps around the track to see if they can succeed. Some will and some won't, those that do go on to race again. Those that don't make it are quickly pulled aside and, once the lessons are learned, are quickly stripped of any further resources. The objective is to find out fast - before too much money, time or other resources have been expended. The many growth opportunities available to the organization must compete against each other to win the backing of senior management and the commitment of the company. But an important point to note is that there is no stigma to bowing out early. That is important because if an opportunity cannot win the internal race for investment backing or the company's limited resources, then it has little chance of winning in the marketplace. But from the side-lines if can be difficult to determine what the winners will be - it can be a high risk gamble!

Accelerating growth requires identifying and accelerating those new products, segments, strategies or projects capable of racing ahead of the rest of the organization so as to accelerate innovation and well as revenue. It is an approach that requires that the organization accelerate learning and innovation and focus its scarce resources on those opportunities most capable of winning. This is the essence of a dynamic approach to growth strategy favoured by many business writers:

> *'Today's core business is highly unlikely to be an engine of growth for tomorrow'.*
> Rita Gunther McGrath & Ian C. Macmillan[44]

> *How many of our people view this organization not as a set of business units but as a portfolio of core competencies and strategic assets that could be leveraged in new ways, new combinations, or new settings to generate future growth?*
> Rowan Gibson[45]

...relying on the Boston Consulting Group's famous cash cow, which remained the watchword for decades and basically suggests companies squeeze profits from successfully established business, is no longer a guarantee for survival.
Oliver Gassmann, Karolin Frankenberger & Michaela Csik[46]

...leaders of successful and enduring companies make substantial investments not just in near-term performance-related initiatives, but in things that have no clear immediate benefit, nor any cast-iron guarantee that they will pay off at a later date.
Scott Keller & Colin Price[47]

Unrelenting exploitation of small opportunities provide firms with the wherewithal to seize golden opportunities when they arise.
Donald Sull[48]

A successful enterprise usually focuses on becoming increasingly efficient at replicating the same basic things, rather than on becoming equally efficient at doing different things. This was a big factor in the demise of once-great companies like Kodak, Blockbuster, and Nokia.
Rowan Gibson[49]

SUMMARY: NEED FOR SPEED

Do you feel the need for speed in your organization? If you are like most managers the answer is 'YES'. That means you want your organization to go (and indeed grow) faster. Accelerating growth isn't easy however, especially if that growth is to be sustained and profitable over time.

How fast you can go depends on what type of revenue generating/value creating machine you are driving and the shape that it is in. It also depends on where you are on the starting grid. That is not to say that the driver does not matter, but whether your vehicle is a Porsche or a bus sets the real parameters for speed and performance.

Your organization may have several vehicles for growth – the equivalent of a number of cars in different races. This is an application of the portfolio approach to strategy. The question is: What vehicles are capable of accelerating sustained and profitable growth? That is capable of F1™ levels of acceleration.

When it comes to the racetrack that is your industry or marketplace there are vehicles of every class. Although many are capable of reaching high speeds and doing a number of fast laps, most don't have the speed and agility to win consistently over the longer term. Indeed, only about one in ten organizations are capable of Formula One™ levels of performance. That requires triple acceleration; growing the top line, bottom line and ROA by at least 5.5% over a decade. But achieving this also requires accelerating value creation, innovation, skills and a lot more besides.

Where will growth come from – will it be derived from the core, or from the edges of your organization? The ability to devise 'a balanced portfolio' of strategic growth experiments is key. That requires fast laps.

Section 3

METAPHOR FOR GROWTH

A metaphor is a weapon of mass understanding.

Anne Miller [50]

INTRODUCTION

You need greater innovation, fresh thinking and creative problem solving in respect of your organization's growth. But first you will need to change the way that your team talks and indeed thinks about its performance.

Planning and executing on strategies for growth requires more than scenarios and spreadsheets. It requires new levels of engagement and insight. So, take the first step by changing the language as well as imagery used in discussions around growth.

The objective of this section is to infuse your organization's next conversation about growth, strategy and change with words such as; passion, speed, competition and, of course winning.

MIND YOUR LANGUAGE

Parse the content of your next management meeting - the items on the agenda, the text on any slides or documents and in particular the words used in the discussion: How motivational or inspiring is the language, the images or metaphors used? How well does it engage all of those involved?

While the need for speed in most organizations is great, the traditional language and indeed imagery used often hinders an effective dialog about performance and potential. It also limits the effectiveness of the plans that are written and the workshops and away-days that shape them.

When it comes to growth; innovation, creativity and fresh thinking are as important as the more traditional tasks, such as; running the numbers, building scenarios and writing strategic plans. Yet it is all too easy to get stuck in our thinking. The tendency is to approach problems in the same old ways – with the same standard agendas, planning processes, or strategy away days. But, to paraphrase Einstein, "today's business performance problems won't be solved by the same thinking that created them." A first step to solving today's problems is to change the way we talk about them. Indeed, changing how managers think and talk about growth is key to innovation in respect of new strategies, as well as new products and new markets. It requires breaking free of the limitations of the traditional language, images and metaphors in respect of business growth and performance.

OLD WAYS OF TALKING ABOUT GROWTH

This is a book about accelerating growth and what it takes to compete and to win in quickening markets. That makes it a book about business strategy and organizational change, but with one big difference; the language and imagery used. Take the words for example:

Competitive advantage	Core Competencies
Core Competence	Diversification
Diversification	Portfolio Management
Segmentation	Market Attractiveness &
Differentiation	Amenability
Strategic Intent	Market Entry Strategy
Strategic Vision	Dogs, Stars, Cash Cows, etc.
Strategic Focus	Strategic Inflection
Strategic Ambition	Situational Analysis
Strategic Leadership	Strategic Goals
Market Strategy	Strategic Positioning
Product Strategy	Product Life Cycle
Strategic Business Unit	Strategic Alliance
Mission	Strategic Alignment
Organizational Change	Dynamic Strategy

Written about by academics and consultants, rather than managers, areas such as strategy have developed their own language - complete with buzzwords and jargon. But use the words from the table in your next meeting and watch how quickly eyes will glaze over. The problem is that while managers need to be more strategic, that does not mean that they have to become less plain speaking. Too many discussions about growth are hindered by the language used - it limits not just the dialog, but also the creativity, problem solving and innovation of all those involved.

> *Business and management science has become a world in itself, and the language of business has become increasingly technical, introverted, and coded.*
> Christian Madsbjerg & Mikkel B. Rasmussen[51]

OUT-DATED METAPHORS

It is not just a problem of language, the imagery or metaphors used in discussing business or strategy don't help either. In particular, the three most widely used metaphors to be found in business books struggle to be relevant in an era of accelerating change – these are; ancient warriors, the battlefield and the chess player.

(a) Ancient Warriors

Many industries have been transformed in less than a decade, yet for more than two millennia after his death the warrior Sun Tzu lives on in many of today's business strategy books. Not surprisingly however it is difficult for the writings of a warrior from times past to teach managers about competing in the age of the web, global markets and continuous innovation.

(b) The Battlefield

The word 'strategy' may have its origins in the battlefield moves of generals, but despite being so widely quoted what can von Clausewitz, a general of the Napoleonic Wars, say to managers in this modern era? Most of today's thought-leaders on business strategy and performance have dispensed with the battlefield metaphor because 'business, unlike a war or battle, is not primarily about defeating an enemy'[52]. Today's focus is more on creating value, rather than waging war.

(c) The Art of Chess

Chess has long been a popular metaphor for business planning and strategy. For example, the images of chess board and pensive chess player are to be found on the cover pages of many strategy books. Yet, chess speaks little to the demands of competing in fast changing markets. Rather it resonates with slower times, when solitary managers could ponder at length over the next move and when thinking logically /analytically was all there was to success.

Strategy Pre-2014

It was a solitary left-brained activity: analytical, cautious & slow. Just like chess!

As Slow As A Game of Chess!

If conventional business is like chess with a two-minute timer for each move, Internet businesses are like speed chess, with a fifteen-second timer.
Mark Gottfredson[53]

The traditional metaphors of business have little or no relevance to competing in a dynamic modern business arena that demands collaboration, innovation and agility.

The Power of Metaphor

Whenever one thing is described in terms of another, that's a metaphor. For example, if you are hungry you might say that you could 'eat a horse' or if you feel your efforts are futile you might say that you are 'flogging a dead horse'. But metaphors are not just a matter of words or language. Research tells us that effective use of metaphors has the power to engage new thinking, access the emotions and to spur creativity.[54] Even more exciting are the findings that metaphors don't just reveal our thinking – they shape our experiences. This offers the tantalizing prospect that changing the metaphors we use can change our reality (as we experience it)[55]. The implication for managers is: How you and your team talk about growth or performance and in particular the metaphors and models used matter. This revelation spurred our search for a new metaphor and language around business growth, strategy and organizational change.

> 'If the planners had once thought their job was delivering information to decision makers, it was now clear that their task was to help managers rethink their worldview'.
> Peter M. Senge[56]

WHY LANGUAGE REALLY MATTERS

In the past you might be inclined to think that the choice of language or metaphor (Samurai warrior or a battlefield general) didn't really matter. However, the work of psychologists in recent years tells us otherwise.

It is now clear that the language and imagery used shapes our attitudes and behaviors around any topic and the topic of growth is no different.

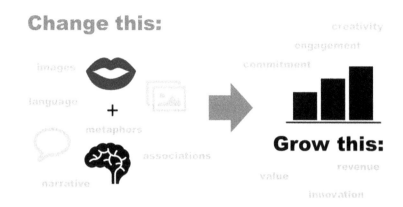

Changing the language around your strategy for growth is an important element of changing the strategy itself[57]. Thus began our quest for a new metaphor – one that would resonate with the challenges faced by today's managers, including; fast changing markets, quick moving competitors and ever more demanding customers.

> *It's not so much that we talk about the world as we see it, it's more that we see the world as we talk about it. When we change the patterns of talk or conversation, we change the world.*
> Sarah Passmore, Jonathan Cantore & Stefan Lewis[58]

YOUR TEAM'S GROWTH MIND-SET

There is a psychology to growth. That is to say what goes on in the heads of mangers and their teams matter. It has a major impact on the success of the strategy to exploit any market opportunity. However, the mind-set generally gets little consideration in management books, or conference papers. Perhaps that is not surprising after all it is a lot more difficult to measure and even to manage than factors such as; competitive strategy, product – market fit, core competence and most of the other factors linked to accelerated growth.

> Talk is key to the executive's work . . . the use of language to shape new possibilities, reframe old perspectives, and excite new commitments . . .
> Juanita Brown, David Isaacs, et al.[59]

To discover your organization's growth mind-set, you need to listen to your team's internal narrative. This narrative is important in understanding behaviour. Moreover, changing the narrative is important if the mind-set, behaviour and results are to change[60].

> In today's complicated and uncertain environment the greatest dangers are... in our own minds - our inability to see our own limits and to see things differently.
> Yoram Wind and Colin Crooke[61]

SEEKING A NEW METAPHOR

Our search for a more contemporary and meaningful metaphor for today's business environment began by writing out the key messages or themes related to accelerating sustained and profitable growth as identified by our research. They included:

1. Accelerating growth - sustainable profitable growth.
2. Speed, urgency, agility and dynamism.
3. Competitive advantage, out-manoeuvring and overtaking the competition.
4. Drive, skill, passion, purpose and desire to win.
5. Strategy meets action, market intelligence, dynamic market fit, and market traction.
6. Great teamwork, high-performing teams, shared definition of success, interdependence and cross-functional collaboration.

7. High-performance, maximizing potential, leading the pack, winning, etc.

8. Relentless innovation, continuous improvement, excellence, pushing the boundaries or performing on / at the edge.

How to find a metaphor that would communicate most, if not all, of these things? The answer came one Sunday afternoon watching television. There it was on display before thousands of spectators and fans and broadcast to many millions more. It involved:

- Intense competitive rivalry.
- Incredible speed combined with agility.
- A burning obsession with winning, combined with great skill.
- Continuous improvement and the quest for a millisecond advantage.
- Teamwork par excellence.

It was F1™ – the Monaco Grand Prix to be precise.   The perfect metaphor for the requirements of accelerating sustainable growth.

> *Since we have a hard time visualizing something unfamiliar, we instead take a word or concept we are familiar with and recast it into an unknown or abstract concept. We understand new things by comparing them to things we already know.*
> Christian Madsbjerg & Mikkel B. Rasmussen[62]

A NEW METAPHOR FOR GROWTH

Ask managers to list the key words they associate with Formula One™ and you find that most of them apply in business. The diagram overleaf is an example – the larger the word, the more often it was mentioned.

It is uncanny how this list relates to the challenges of accelerating growth within an organization. Innovation, technology, strategy, and competition to name just a few – they are all there. Also there are passion, teamwork and agility. Clearly winning on the racetrack and winning in the boardroom have a lot in common.

> Q: How many of the F1™-related words apply to your organization, business unit or team? Circle them in the diagram above. Which ones are missing?

Pretty much every manager wants these words to be associated with their organization, business unit or team. But for this to happen they need to enter the everyday conversation of the organization. Managers need to be talking more about; competition, speed, passion, talent and teamwork. Most important of all, in an increasingly demanding marketspace, they need to be continually talking about winning. Is this the case in your organization?

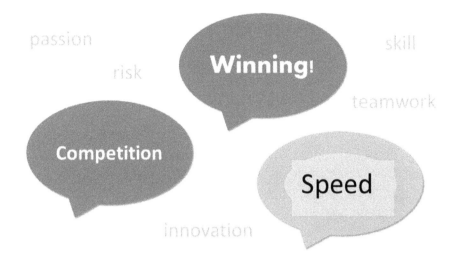

The demands on your organization in terms of speed, agility and innovation have grown dramatically in line with an accelerating pace of market change, more aggressive competitors and increasingly demanding customers. The message of the F1™ metaphor is to be faster, more agile and more innovative. To be the F1™ of your industry.

> F1™ is where all the fantastic drivers are, so you just don't know how good you are until you get there.
> Jean Alesi[63]

It is a cue to start talking (and thinking) about competition, speed and most of all winning. If these words dominated your management meetings, workshops and away days the level of energy and innovation around growth would get a major boost. The technical term is Cognitive Re-framing[64] and it holds that until you change how people see or talk and think about something little else will change.

> Organizations need to find new ways of responding to adaptive challenges. They need to get comfortable with ambiguity and seek insight from a broader range of places. They need to continuously frame and reframe not only their answers but also the questions they pose.
> Chris Ertel & Lisa Kay Solomon[65]

COGNITIVE RE-FRAMING

Many of the limits to growth and performance are to be found in the way we think and talk about the subject. That makes re-framing the conversation about growth vitally important.

Why Re-framing?
Because many of the limits to growth and performance are to be found here!

You don't have to be a racing fan to appreciate the speed and technical sophistication of a F1™ racing car. But even if you don't, the simple yet effective comparisons drawn between acceleration on the racetrack and accelerating business growth won't be lost on you. The message of F1™ is you can always go faster, be more agile and more innovative. It is a powerful message for managers and teams.

The Pinnacle of Speed

Fast growth companies belong to an exclusive and prestigious club. These clubs have different names, such as; the Inc. 500, Fortune's Fastest Growing, Deloitte Technology Fast 500, Forbes Fast Tech, or regionally the Philadelphia 100 or Chicago Fast Fifty. Outside the USA these clubs have different names, such as Germany's Growth Champions, Canada's Profit 500 or the UK's Fast Track 100. We describe these companies and those who desire to join them as Fit for F1™. They are an elite prestigious and speed-obsessed group - just like those to be found at the pinnacle of motor sports.

ARE YOU FIT FOR F1™?

Do you want to be among your industry's highest performers – leading the way in terms of passion, innovation and of course in terms of sustained and profitable growth?   That is to be in the F1™ of your industry.

Are You

Fit for F1™

In Your Industry?

Why be in F1™? In more and more industries simply being good at product innovation, management, marketing or operations isn't enough anymore. That may have been fine 5, 10 or 15 years ago, but every year the bar is set a little higher. Sticking with last year's definition of good means you are at risk of falling behind.   The warnings are plentiful:

> 'A warning to execs: At the present rate of churn rate, 75% of the S&P 500 will be replaced by 2027'.
> Innosight[66]

> ...the tension between what it takes to stay ahead of increasingly fierce competition, on the one hand, and needing to deliver this year's results, on the other, can be overwhelming.
> John P. Kotter[67]

To sustain growth it is important to realize that what worked last year will not necessarily work next year; an organization that wants to manage growth successfully needs to change things that are not yet broken.
Rupert Merson[68]

The biggest single danger for market leaders is falling into what we call "satisfactory underperformance." ...You ought to have a solid leadership position not only in market share but in cost, quality, and customer loyalty. If you don't achieve your full potential, you are underperforming. You are also vulnerable to attack.
Mark Gottfredson[69]

Organizational decline is inevitable unless leaders prepare for change – even when standing at the pinnacle of success.
James Kerr[70]

...it is crucial to question the pillars of today's success and mentally prepare yourself for your company's demise, even if it's doing famously right now. We live in an era of temporary competitive advantage: success can only be maintained if its roots are continually re-examined and nurtured.
Oliver Gassmann, Karolin Frankenberger & Michaela Csik[71]

...the most creative, successful business leaders... question the conventional wisdom of their industry, the fundamental practices of their company, even the validity of their own assumptions.
Warren Berger[72]

The often repeated message is – don't get complacent – there is no standing still. Companies have to be good to belong to the vanguard of their industry - to be listed among the Fortune 500, or listed on the NYSE - for example. They have to have good products, good managers and satisfied customers. But is that enough to accelerate sustained and profitable growth in a fast changing and increasingly turbulent world? The lesson of Blockbuster, Nokia and Kodak suggest it isn't. Good is no longer enough. It is not just poorly managed companies that fall behind - it happens to good companies too! It happens to well-managed companies - companies with good strategies, good products and satisfied customers. Many longer established and larger organizations are juggernauts suited to the motorway of a mature established and relatively stable marketplace. But in a fast changing marketplace they are at risk of being out-maneuvered by competitors and overtaken by technological, societal or other changes. They are not quite fit for F1™.

> *Most companies with a practiced discipline of listening to their best customers and identifying new products that promise greater profitability and growth are rarely able to build a case for investing in disruptive technologies until it is too late.*
> Clayton Christensen[73]

What Kind of Car are You?

"We are not a F1™ car!" exclaimed one executive. She quickly added, "As a car we are more like a Batmobile!" There were several laughs and a few raised eyebrows.

But suddenly everybody was listening intently as the manager started to explain: "Just like Batman's car we have lots of buttons, knobs and gadgets. That's how our customers see us and more specifically our products – lots of gadgets and gimmicks." She concluded with the message, "We need to simplify our products, focus on those core features required by the customer and do them really well."

This is an example of how engaging the F1™ metaphor leads to greater creativity and a more powerful dialog.

STRIVE FOR F1™ PERFORMANCE

The message is; don't just settle for being a good company, why not strive for more? That is to be great – to be extra-ordinary. To have extraordinary products, service, employees, innovation and so on. In the language of this book - set your sights on being the F1™ of your industry. The requirement of winning on the race track; speed, agility, innovation and so on are also the requirements of winning in fast changing markets. Again F1™'s message for managers is; you can always go faster, be more agile and more innovative.

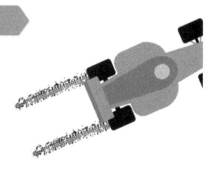

(and your organization)

Can **you** be more:

- Agile?
- Dynamic?
- Responsive?
- Innovative?
- Passionate?
- Brave?

...oh and Faster too!

Being in F1™ is more demanding than almost any other arena in terms of technology, skill, spectators and competition. It is the pinnacle of achievement - it takes winning to the next level. It is a high pressure environment, more expensive and more dangerous. But for those who make it to F1™ the rewards are great; prestige, glamour and riches. It is the level of passion, excitement and thrill that managers and teams should experience. The question is: Are you fit for F1™?

Be *FASTER*, more *agile*

& more innovative.

Be the...

 **of your industry!**

> This growth mindset is based on the belief that your basic qualities are things you can cultivate through your efforts. Although people may differ in every which way—in their initial talents and aptitudes, interests, or temperaments—everyone can change and grow through application and experience.
> Carol Dweck[74]

Unlocking Your Creativity

The Growth Pitstop™ metaphor has been designed to engage managers in a new level of creative problem-solving in respect of business strategy. As managers we are all admonished to be more creative and innovative. Names such as Elon Musk and the late Steve Jobs are held up as role models – an impossible standard to match! Yet we are told that deep within us all are levels of entrepreneurial leadership and creativity equal to those that created eBay or the iPhone[75]. Even the most 'linear-thinking spreadsheet-using' of us has the native ability to access deep levels of creativity and innovation[76].

> Contrary to popular belief, innovation is not some mystical art that's forbidden to mere mortals.
> Rowan Gibson[77]

The Growth Pitstop™ doesn't simply repeat the calls for innovation and creativity. Rather it has been constructed in a way that makes such calls redundant. Simply read on and follow the exercises, without doing anything else you will have engaged a new level of creative problem-solving in respect of your strategy for growth.

> *...even in the midst of extreme uncertainty, business leaders rarely diverge from default thinking.*
> Christian Madsbjerg & Mikkel B. Rasmussen[78]

If you are going to be in F1™ you need a high performance Revenue Generating / Value Creating Machine (Section 5). You need to pitstop regularly (Section 6) and of course a great pit crew (Section 7).

> *...there are many factors that can influence the lack of performance of a driver, such as the design of the car and effectiveness of the race team. Equally, there are many factors that explain the apparent success of a driver rather than just driving skills.*
> Mark Jenkins, Ken Pasternak & Richard West[79]

SUMMARY

Discussions about growth are often hindered by the traditional language and indeed imagery used. The first step to greater creativity and innovation is to change the way your team talks about the opportunities and challenges it faces.

Your managers need to be talking more about competition, speed, passion, talent and teamwork. Most important of all, in an increasingly demanding marketspace, your teams need to be continually talking about winning. They need to talk and indeed think about growth as if they were in F1™.

Formula One™ is about speed, agility and competition. It is also about passion and skill. But most of all it is about winning. These are also part of the formula for success in any fast growing business. If these words dominated your management meetings, workshops and away days the level of energy and innovation around growth would get a major boost.

Do you want to be among your industry's highest performers – leading the way in terms of passion, innovation and of course in terms of sustained and profitable growth?   That is to be in the F1™ of your industry.

The message for managers is; you can always go faster, be more agile and more innovative.

> *Effective scaling depends on believing and living a shared mind-set throughout your group, division, or organization.*
> Robert I. Sutton & Huggy Rao[80]

Inspired by F1™?

If you want to learn more about the inspiration that managers can gain from F1™ we would recommend Mark Gallagher's Book: 'The Business of Winning: Strategic Success from the Formula One Track to the Boardroom' (Kogan Page, 2014). Also if you would like to understand the dynamics of success in racing 'Race to Win' by Derek Daly and Mario Andretti (Octane Press, 2013) or Neil Robert's 'Think Fast' (CreateSpace, 2010) are a great read.

> *"Formula 1 is the best. And we don't need anything in it that isn't the best.*
> Bernie Ecclestone[81]

Section 4

FORMULA FOR GROWTH™

*A racing car is an animal with
a thousand adjustments.*

Mario Andretti[82]

INTRODUCTION

Accelerating growth is complex, sustaining it is more complex still. The solution to the challenge of sustained profitable growth is not going to be found in any one function, nor in any new management fad. It is not about doing one thing, but doing many things and doing all of them better. In short it requires a formula.

Formula One™ owes its name to the formula or set of rules that govern winning in the world's most competitive sport. But what are the rules for competing in the world's most competitive markets? If only they were published together in one place - like those that govern the racetrack – that would really help managers to win. That is the objective of this section; a Formula for Growth™ setting out the driver, team and car (or strategy) requirements of accelerating sustained and profitable growth.

HOW TO ACCELERATE GROWTH?

How do you measure an organization, its management team or CEO? Well it's quite simple: Growth – **sustained and profitable revenue growth**. But how to accelerate such growth? More specifically:

- Can it be achieved by your core business or elsewhere?
- Will it be delivered by existing or new products?
- Will it require entering new markets or market segments?
- Are there channels that can deliver accelerated growth?
- What manpower and other resources will be required?
- What systems and processes will be required for growth?
- What should the strategy for growth look like?
- What talent or resources will be required?

There are of course many more questions when it comes to the issue of growth. That is not surprising really given the complexity of the topic.

GROWTH IS COMPLEX

Growing a business is complex, growing in a sustainable and profitable way is even more challenging still. Indeed, you could argue that it is every bit as complex as physics or chemistry, only more unpredictable because there are fewer scientific laws and the results depend on the people involved (e.g. your customers, your sales and marketing people, your supply chain team, and your competitor's people too). One of the implications is that growing a business cannot be reduced to one or two factors.

Growing a business is every bit as **complex is physics or chemistry**. Only more unpredictable. It cannot be reduced to one or two factors.

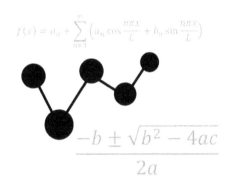

The solution to accelerating sustained and profitable growth won't be found in any one business function, discipline or management topic. It won't be found in the latest management fad either. The solution is not just about leadership, innovation, sales/marketing or strategy. It is about all of these things and many more besides.

> *Business may not be rocket science, but it is complex. You and your competitors have an infinite number of moves and countermoves at your disposal, and it's always hard to see out beyond the next few moves.*
> Christian Madsbjerg & Mikkel B. Rasmussen[83]

Sustained profitable growth is generated as the result of the combined efforts of multiple business functions including Operations, Customer Service and Finance, as well as the traditional revenue-generating functions of sales and marketing. Growth is cross-functional and multi-disciplinary.

> *...the growth of these companies (successful startups with extraordinary growth) did not come from traditional marketing. In fact many jettisoned their Vice Presidents of Marketing in favor of cross-functional growth teams that included individuals from engineering, product, sales, and marketing.*
>
> Sean Ellis & Morgan Brown[84]

A FORMULA FOR GROWTH™

Because growth is complex it requires a formula. It is not binary - not a 0 or 1. It is not the result of a single factor, a strategy, decision or skill, but rather the result of a multiplicity of factors – all interlinked and interconnected.

formula

Noun / **for·mu·la** / plural: **formulas** or **formulae**)

...a plan, method or procedure for achieving something.
...a recipe or prescription ...a list of ingredients.
...a mathematical relationship...

 $\sqrt{a^2 + b^2}$

Synonyms: *Recipe, blueprint, prescription, method, plan, technique, system, rules, principles, precepts*

Merriam Webster / Dictionary.com / Oxford Dictionary

The dictionary defines a formula as 'a plan, method or procedure for achieving something' – think of a mathematical formula for example. It can also be 'a recipe, prescription or list of ingredients.' This is important because there is a multiplicity of things that must happen right across the organization to accelerate revenue in a sustained and profitable manner. The number and complexity of these factors explains why sustained profitable growth eludes so many companies.

There is another use of the term 'Formula' that has relevance to this book – it is Formula One™. That is the 140 or so pages of sporting and technical regulations issued by the FIA and setting out how races are to be run and cars are to be constructed.

Formula One

The 'Formula' is 142 pages of FIA **rules** with which racing cars must comply, incl:

Engine   Chassis   Tyres   Fuel   Safety   Rules

You cannot win if you don't adhere to the formula.

The Formula in F1™ sets out the rules that govern success on the race track. Race teams no matter how fast they go cannot win if they don't adhere to the formula. The question is what are the rules that govern how fast, how profitably and for how long your organization can grow? In other words: What is your Formula for Growth™?

> To generate a steady growth in revenue, you must have an identified and replicable framework, which becomes a model for consistency and sustainable success.

Christopher Ryan, Nate Warren & Gail Carson[85]

MILES OF RESEARCH

Understanding what separates the fast from the slow is the foundational knowledge that equips managers to accelerate the growth of their own organizations, business units and teams. However, most busy managers don't have time to read all the various research reports, books or publications on the subject. There is simply too much! For example, in the area of 'strategy' alone Amazon™ has almost 70,000 books on the subject, while Google™ has 641 million web pages. One of our speed-obsessed colleagues did the following calculation: If you took the pages written about strategy (in published books and online) and put them end to end they would stretch so far that you would have to drive at 62mph without stopping for 82.4 days in order to reach the last page.

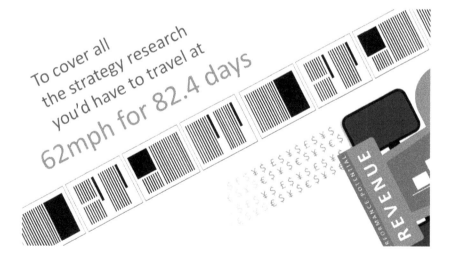

Driving a F1™ car would reduce that figure to a little over 20 days, which is interesting as our objective is to enable managers to more speedily access the latest research on the topic of business growth.

MODELLING GROWTH

As managers regularly remind us they live in an age of executive summaries and soundbites. Even if they had time to read lots of books and research papers, much of it would be quickly forgotten. That presents a problem when it comes to some of the more thorough or scientific research into the requirements for growth. There is lots of text, quite a few statistics and a list of research citations. While there are occasional graphs, or models to break up the text, it tends to be relatively hard going.

Decades of research in the business arena has resulted in many great models or tools to help managers to measure and manage the performance of their organizations, business units and teams. These models are an important means of managing the complexity of the subject of growth.

> *...I flick the pages and look at the pictures. If I see no diagrams, no graphs and no models I can usually make an accurate prediction that the book is of the old school.*
> Neill Rackham[86]

TIME TO RE-MODEL?

Models are important. They are a visual representation of a complex subject, theory or idea aimed at making it easier for people to comprehend and communicate. For expansive topics such as strategy, innovation and growth a model is essential. But it can be a challenge to make business models engaging.

> *'A simple visual image is one of the best ways to help a group see the same thing at the same time. It can dramatically decrease the time to reach insights and come to agreement.'*
> *J C Spender & Bruce A Strong, 'Strategic Conversations'*[87]

Modelling Business Performance: Here is a selection of some of the best and most familiar models. How many of them do you recognize?

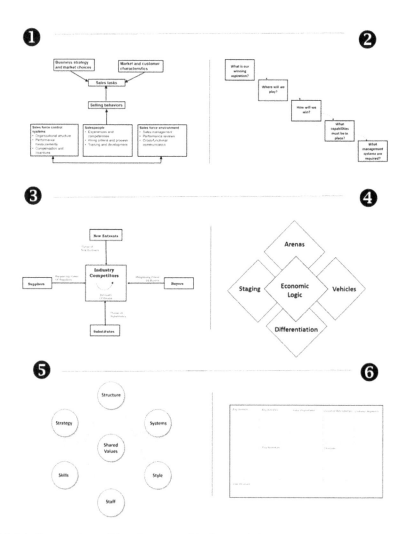

Match the number of the diagram with the model:

_ Aligning Sales & Strategy (Cespedes)   _ Diamond Model
_ Business Canvass (Ostewalder & Pigneur)   _ Porter's 5 Forces
_ Playing to Win Model (Lafley & Martin)   _ Mc Kinsey's 7 Ss

To check your answers go to the end of this section.

> *A simple visual image is one of the best ways to help a group see the same thing at the same time. Many of the most influential ideas in the field of strategy have been expressed in memorable visual frameworks.*
> Chris Ertel & Lisa Kay Solomon[88]

While most models don't require a graphics department, their straight lines and square boxes often struggle to fire up the imagination. It is difficult for abstracted models to come to life – to enter the conversation and change the narrative. They rarely convey any meaning other than that which is given to them and they need to be explained. With this in mind we set about creating a different type of model – one that was designed for Generations X, Y and Z - a model for managers, not scientists or academics. We wanted to do for business models what the Apple iPhone™ did for mobile phones. That is make them a lot more user-friendly and engaging.

There are lots of models with straight lines **and** square boxes, we wanted one that was self-evident & easier to remember.

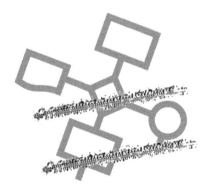

> *Systems of deduction and computation do not produce new interesting ideas, no matter how hard one winds the crank.*
> Richard P. Rumelt[89]

MODELLING FOR GENERATIONS X AND Y

In building a next-generation model of business performance we wanted a picture that would paint a thousand words, and in such a wordy area as business strategy and growth that was particularly important. We wanted something that was **visual, easy to grasp and that directly related to the issue of accelerating growth**. We wanted a model that would communicate without many words and across cultures – it would need to convey metaphoric or symbolic meaning. In short we wanted science, but communicated with power and simplicity.

> *'If I can't picture it. I can't understand it'*
> *Albert Einstein[90]*

We were seeking to create a powerful visual model that was intuitive, easy to remember and capable of being communicated without any special knowledge or training. Oh and one further challenge, it would need to engage the many managers who had little interest in either strategy or what were seen as the traditional revenue generating functions of sales and marketing. So while our statisticians and analysts gathered the data to make a robust model for accelerating business performance, we put our more creative brains to work on how it might be communicated or represented most effectively.

> *Don't presume that business and managing can be reduced to a quantitative science.*
> J.-C. Spender & Bruce A. Strong[91]

As was said in the last section it stands to reason that when everything else in business is changing so fast – technology, competition, markets and so on – that the language, imagery and models of business must change too. With this in mind any new model would need to connect with and communicate competition, speed and winning, as with the metaphor of Formula One™ racing. With the design specification created we let the graphic designers off to do their work. With surprising speed they came back to us with the key requirements met, even surpassed. The key accelerators of growth shown in a model that communicates competition, speed and winning at its core. A model in the shape of a race car, driver and pit team – as shown overleaf.

WHAT DO YOU SEE?

What do you see in the model? There is a fast car, with a driver seated in the middle, and surrounded by a pit team actively making the required adjustments to keep the car in the race and maximize its chances of winning. The car of course is your company's strategy for growth. How fast your strategy will really go however depends on the people that build, drive and support it.

F1™ racing is about having a great driver, a great car and – last but not least – having a great pit crew focused on helping the car and the driver to win. **Replace the word 'car' with 'revenue-generating machine'** and the same applies in business. The formula is a vehicle (no pun intended!) for communicating some of the most exhaustive research undertaken into the factors that accelerate growth. There are a total of 17 parts as labelled in the diagram and they relate to the car, the driver and the team. Each of these parts has lots of sub-components – being made up of a total of 248 variables that have been scientifically linked to accelerating business performance and are measured via an online predictive growth analysis (see Appendix). In this way the approach is very similar to that in F1™ where sensors around the car send data back to the team during the race regarding every aspect of performance.

> *'Strategic thinkers construct— and constantly tinker with— mental models about how their business works to solve problems and spot new opportunities.'*
> Chris Ertel and Lisa Kay Solomon[92]

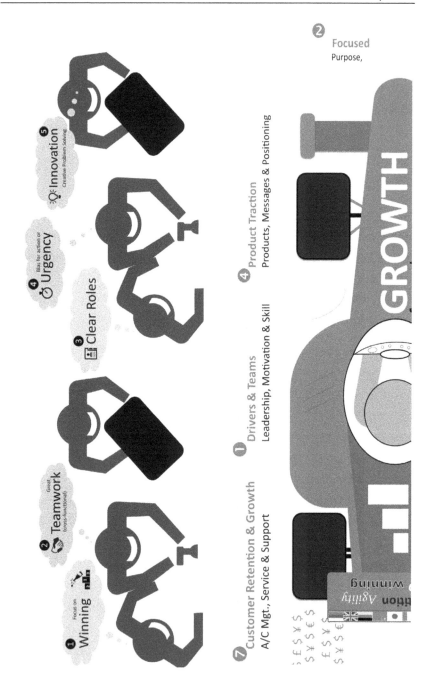

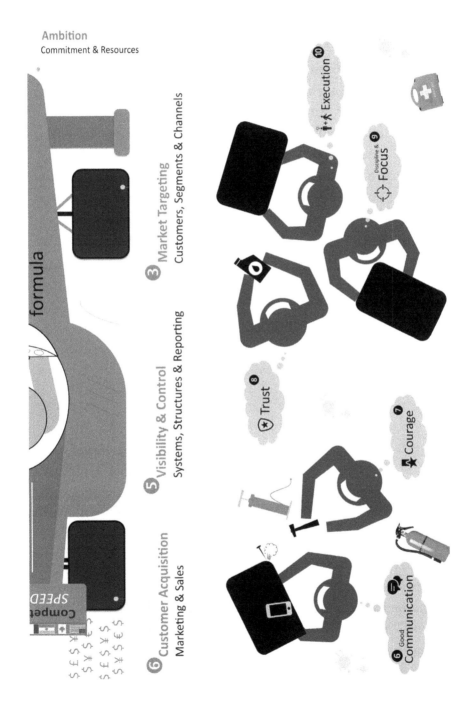

IT'S NOT JUST A PERFORMANCE MODEL

The Formula for Growth™ is a sophisticated performance equation, based on lots of variables. But our research team are always keen to point out that it is not just a model of performance. Although it is a powerful tool for understanding performance and in particular making sense of under-performance, the primary purpose is to look forward, rather than backwards. The formula's key role is to facilitate a debate about the potential for future growth and to focus attention on those factors that can accelerate and sustain profitable growth into the future. It focuses executives on the key question of strategy: How to make the car go faster?

STRATEGY IS:
How to Make the Car
Go Faster?

If the race has been run it is important to understand what happened and to learn from it, but there is little point in dwelling on it. It is more empowering and more motivational to focus on the road ahead. What is done is done, all management can control is what happens next. So when groups interact with the formula in Growth Pitstop™ workshops the conversation focuses on 'how can we make the car/organization go/grow faster. While you will hear people say 'we are not good at this' or 'this is slowing us down' – as they highlight areas that are underperforming we recommend steering the conversation towards discussing 'how can we go or grow faster?' In this way the formula provides a means of increasing performance to the level of an organization or team's potential.

> *Good visuals can dramatically decrease the time it takes people*
> *to reach insights and come to agreement.*
> Chris Ertel & Lisa Kay Solomon[93]

Accelerating the 7S Model

Of the models available to guide managers in the process of setting and accelerating strategy the McKinsey 7S is among the most popular. The 7s of course stand for; strategy, systems, structure, style, staff, skills and shared values. It is, as its creators intended, a great way to look at organizational effectiveness[94]. However as further evidence of the accelerated rate of change the McKinsey 7S is fast approaching its 40 birthday. With that in mind the Formula for Growth™ is aimed at taking the 7S up to speed. Reflecting in particular the dramatic shifts in technology, markets and so on.

> *Today these graphics and schematic representations –*
> *flowcharts, process, etc. – are widespread…, but at the time, it*
> *(the 7S) was a stroke of genius…*
> Anne-Christine Cadiat[95]

PERFORMANCE = MODEL & METAPHOR

Few, if any, of the parts of the formula will come as a surprise to you. Most have been linked to business success for a long time and written about in many different books, journals and blogs. What is unusual is to have such an array of factors presented in a single model – also one that looks very different to what has come before. The formula brings all the factors linked to growth together in one place in order to reveal the full complexity and the multiplicity of factors involved (ranging from leadership to strategy), as well as how they are interconnected. It is built on a scientific assessment and algorithm which predicts the ability to accelerate sustained profitable growth by measuring the 248 growth related variables (within the formula) for any organization, business unit or team.

> *...without a new and unique insight at the end of it our strategizing efforts are in vain.*
> Kees van der Heijden[96]

As a model the formula fits into the same class as Porter's 5 Forces or the BCG Matrix - it is a scientifically grounded tool of analysis. Where it is different is its visual presentation - it trades the straight lines and square boxes of most models for something that is visually more interesting and more memorable. This is aimed at facilitating new thinking, as well as creative problem solving in respect of strategy. By integrating the imagery of F1™ and the 17 factors in the formula we have both a metaphor and a model – think of it as a **meta-model** – that combines the power of a metaphor with the clarity of a model. In other words it can communicate meaning and emotion though associations, but with few words. In this case the associations with speed, competition, skill and most of all winning.

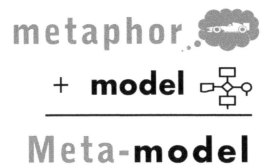

The Formula for Growth™ is a model and a metaphor aimed at re-framing the requirements of growth in a way that facilitates new thinking - or to be more precise; breakthrough thinking. That requires more than technical information, tables and statistics about growing, or indeed going; fast. It requires a framework for creative problem solving around growth, strategy and innovation.

> *...if you want to teach people a new way of thinking, don't bother trying to teach them. Instead given them a tool, the use of which will lead to new ways of thinking.*
> Buckminster Fuller[97]

COMBINING 'HARD' AND 'SOFT'

The formula is the perfect balance of man/woman and machine or what is often called 'the hard' and 'the soft' when it comes to accelerating growth as shown in the diagram overleaf. It is a total success equation.

The 'hard' parts of the formula describe how the strategy works, including structures, systems and processes. They are represented by the car (or revenue generating machine as on the left of the diagram) at the center of the model and account for 7 of the 17 parts of the formula.

the 'hard'
Strategies, Structures, Systems, Processes, etc.

the 'soft'
People, Culture, Behaviors, Ambition, etc.

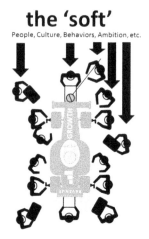

On the 'hard' side of the Formula for Growth™ this book quotes the great work of; Frank Cespedes, JP Kotter, Donald Sull, Chris Zook & James Allen, AG Lafley & Roger L Martin, Henry Mintzberg, Rita Gunter McGrath, Patrick Viguerie, Phil Fernandez, Richard Rumelt, Steve Woods & Alex Shootman to name just a few. We have included quotes and references throughout the book in order to direct you towards their research as follow-on reading.

The people who build, drive and maintain the revenue generating or value creating machine are the 'soft' parts of the formula. Here there are 10 factors related to how effectively these people work together to get the most out of the car (revenue generating / value creating machine) and include the; cross-functional, collaborative, cultural and related aspects of growth. These are often referred to as organizational health and linked directly to the bottom line. Managers who are benchmarked via the pitstop suggest that these account for 40% of growth or success.

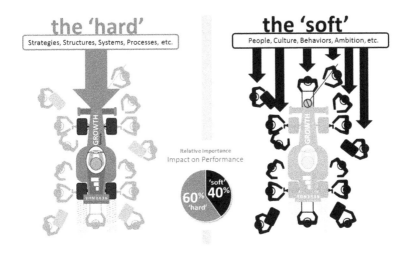

McKinsey data, for example, puts the impact of 'the soft' (using the term organizational health) higher at 53%[98]. But regardless of the precise figure it is clear that you cannot accelerate to top speeds without an effective pit team and the ability to pitstop.

> *...organizations that focused on performance and (organizational) health simultaneously were nearly twice as successful as those that focused on health alone, and nearly three times as successful as those that focused on performance alone.*
> Scott Keller & Colin Price[99]

On the 'soft side' of the Formula for Growth™ this book quotes the great work of; Patrick Lencioni, Garry Hammel, Peter Senge, Margaret J. Wheatley, Robert Kegan and Lisa Laskow Lahey - to name just a few. But the power of the Formula for Growth™ is its integrated view of 'the hard' and 'the soft'. Great organizations – those that enjoy sustained profitable growth – work on the car, the driver and the pit team together. They see all these – hard and soft - as the essential parts of the formula or system that accelerates growth.

To move the car you need to move the people first. A machine has a function, but people have a purpose. To accelerate your revenue generating / value creating machine you must exhilarate the people. That is why managers call priorities around the car (e.g. Market Targeting) 'accelerators'. But when it comes to priorities around the team (e.g. Clear Roles, or Good Communication) they are called 'exhilarators'. The questions is: what are yours?

> *Executives often prioritize strategy, assuming that if they get that right, everything else will fall into place. They think they can ignore their people or, at any rate, treat them as secondary. Bad idea. People are an essential part of any strategy, and regenerating the talent pool is the single most important thing any leader can do to survive and prosper.*
> Sydney Finkelstein[100]

THE REVENUE GENERATING MACHINE

At the center of the meta-model is the Revenue Generating or Value Creating Machine - that is your organization. It is in the form of a high-performance F1™ car – both sleek and fast. This acts as a visual representation of the 7 key variables related to the success of a growth strategy and its execution:

- Focused ambition (Priorities, Resources & Commitment)
- Market Targeting (Customers, Competitors & Channels)
- Product Traction (Products, Messages & Positioning)
- Visibility & Control (Systems, Structures, Reporting & Compliance)
- Customer Acquisition (Sales & Marketing)
- Customer Retention (Account Management, Service & Support)

These seven parts of the car are the mechanics, or nuts and bolts of growth. As you will see from the diagram overleaf these are associated with different parts of the Revenue Generating/Value Creating Machine. For example, visibility and control is the dashboard and controls, while focused ambition is the nose cone of the car.

While we hear managers talk about their Revenue Generating Machine, the formula is about more than top line acceleration. In particular, it addresses the requirements of sustained profitable growth. If the model was simply focused on revenue growth it wouldn't need to be so complex. For example, it would not need to be so pointed in shape and neither the traction of the tires, the sophistication of the controls or the skill of the driver would be so important. Moreover, it could probably be maintained by one or two people, rather than a cross-functional management team. However, as we will explore in later sections the shape of the F1™ racing car and all of the technical innovation behind it stem from the requirements of racing on the most demanding of tracks. In particular, these cars have to be able to accelerate like a rocket when an opening appears, brake from enormous speeds in a matter of meters and stick to the road on sharp corners when the laws of physics suggest that the car should fly off into the air.

> *In the old world managers make products... In the new world managers make sense of things.*
> John Seely Brown[101]

This is a car (revenue generating or value creating machine) for complex and fast changing markets, where competitors are in fast pursuit and the customers or spectators are increasingly demanding. It is a growth vehicle that is designed not just to do a number of fast laps, but to stay the course in order to win the race, as well as the championship.

The Revenue Generating / Value Creating Machine

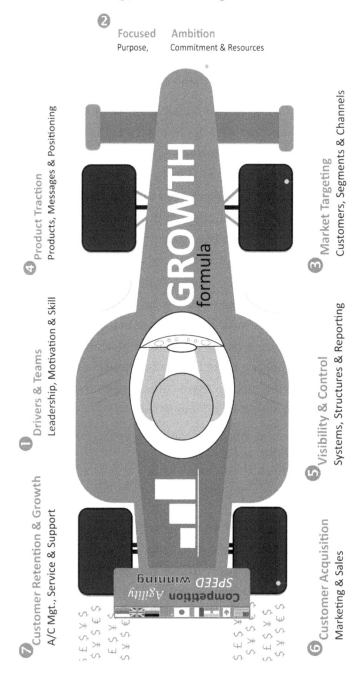

All this makes it the perfect model for accelerating sustained and profitable growth – a revenue generating / value creating machine designed to meet the 5.5% challenge discussed in Section 2: Need for Speed. That is the challenge of sustaining 5.5% growth to the top line, bottom line and return on capital for decade. But it is also a car that delivers maximum thrill to the driver, the team and the spectators (customers and channel partners).

> *More of us agree that growth is about much more than providing a boost to sales, margins, and the bottom line. It is about creating value for all stakeholders; economic value for the shareholders; social value for employees, their families and friends, local communities, and social networks; as well as value for ecosystems and the environment.*
> Tim Jones, Dave McCormick & Caroline Dewing[102]

Your Vehicle for Growth

The Diamond Model of strategy by Don Hambrick and Jim Fredrickson uses the term 'Vehicles' to explore the means of participating in the organization's chosen 'Arenas', incl. internal development, joint venture, licensing/franchising, alliances or acquisitions[103]. The same approach can be applied to the Revenue Generating/Value Creating Machine with any of these 'vehicles' give rise to the strategic issues shown in the Formula for Growth™.

TEAM AND MACHINE

The concept of an organization (or indeed a person) as a machine focuses attention on efficiency and predictability in achieving a particular output, or result. For example, it means thinking of your organization or business unit as a Revenue Generating, or Value Creating Machine (just as you did in Section 2: Need for Speed).

> ...*end goal is always a self-perpetuating machine that is so well oiled, it constantly grows itself.*
> Robert Peters[104]

With a machine there is generally little variability - any of its many parts can be oiled and engineered to optimize performance. However, we don't want you to see your organization as a mere machine where; it can be managed by control, the parts can be seen in isolation of the whole and most of all where people are just cogs.

> *In order for any business to succeed, it must first become a system, so that the business functions exactly the same way every time ...down to the very last detail.*
> Michael Gerber[105]

An organization is more than a machine. Being heavily people-centric it is a lot more complex too. For this reason, the Formula for Growth™ is a mix of team and machine, so to speak. It is the driver, the pit team and the car that wins races. Working on one of these alone is not enough to accelerate the growth of the organization. In this way the formula is aimed at helping you to see your organization - its performance and potential - in all its complexity.

> *...the firm is a money-making machine whose superb design can be sufficient to ensure its long-term viability. But as we know, moth and rust corrupt all worldly things and the firm is a human artifact.*
> J.C. Spender[106]

Sitting quite literally in the middle of the Formula for Growth™ is the driver drawing attention to the factors such as; leadership, motivation, behavior & skill as being central to success. But in racing the driver relies upon a pit team in order to keep the car in the race. In business, as in racing, the performance of the driver and the machine depends on the team that creates, maintains and supports it.

> How do we see a business— as a human community or as a machine for making money?
> Arie Geus[107]

THE 'SOFT' PARTS OF THE FORMULA

The Formula for Growth™ is about fast drivers and fast cars, but of course there is another vital ingredient to winning – pitstops. That is the ability to optimize and repair the car mid-race with lightning speed and efficiency. In racing the best driver in the fastest car doesn't always win the race. Their success is dependent on those who support and service the car, particularly during the heat of the race. That is the pit crew. The precisely-timed millimetre-perfect choreography of a Formula One™ pit crew is the new standard for teamwork. With just seconds separating the winner from the competition, the speed and efficiency of the pit crew is paramount (see Section 7). The same applies in business. Indeed, the ability of your management team to work together effectively is perhaps the ultimate competitive advantage. Of course your team is not working with hydraulic tools, tires and so on. But it does have a racing machine of sorts – a revenue-generating or value-creating machine to optimize and keep in the race.

> ...I see a lot of cars that were created by a group of individuals rather than by a team. The tell-tale sign is an exquisitely optimized part located right next to a block of steel with a hole in it.
> Neil Roberts[108]

Just like the pit team in racing. There are 10 key variables related to the performance of the pit team, as well as the growth of the business. They are shown beside the visual of the soft parts of the formula overleaf as the members of the pit team. These factors are a blend of leadership and culture, as well as organizational health[109] – a measure of the team's desire and ability to accelerate. When we analyse our benchmarking data we can see that the opportunities for acceleration are pretty evenly spread between the car and the pit crew, in terms of the Formula for Growth™. More specifically, the pit crew (examined in Section 7) accounts for 40% of the potential for acceleration, with the car accounting for the rest.

- Focus on Winning

- Teamwork (cross functional)

- Clear Roles

- Urgency (bias for action)

- Good Communication

- Courage

- Trust

- Discipline & Focus

- Execution

- Innovation/Creative Problem Solving

> *"Hard is soft. Soft is hard." That is, it's the plans and the numbers that are often "soft". And the people and shared values and skills which are truly "hard"*
> Tom Peters[110]

Of course the 'hard' and 'soft' is a misnomer, because as most managers know only too well it is the 'soft' that is really the 'hard' part. Machines are predicable, people are not. More importantly all of the variables are interdependent and interrelated. That means you cannot work on one in isolation of another. Just a reductionist view does not work in an area as complex as the growth of an organization.

> *...when we view organizations as living human systems rather than as machines, our beliefs about how to achieve effective organizational change are different. ...it offers a genuinely different way to access and develop the capability of an organization to self-renew and to grow; in other words, to change.*
> Sarah Passmore, Jonathan Cantore & Stefan Lewis[111]

What's Your Key Accelerator?

Managers in an in-company pitstop go to the part of the formula that they feel has the potential to most accelerate growth.

> *...strong strategic thinkers do habitually... Construct— and constantly tinker with— mental models about how their business works to solve problems and spot new opportunities.*
> Chris Ertel & Lisa Kay Solomon[112]

GROWTH REQUIRES SYSTEMS THINKING

A racing car has many parts. An organization is the same and it is how those parts work together that determine the rate of success and level of growth. However, our innate tendency as managers is to focus on some parts more than others. We are like a mechanic with one tool – perhaps it is a spanner or a screwdriver and we keep putting it in the same place. On the other side of the car there is another specialized mechanic with a different tool and putting it in somewhere else. Often nobody is coordinating the effort. But you cannot just fix one part of the car and not pay attention to the others.

> Managers can be like a mechanic with one tool - perhaps it is a spanner or a screwdriver and we keep sticking it in the same place. But what about the rest of the machine?

The Formula for Growth™ is classic systems thinking and requires looking beyond the person or event to the underlying systematic factors that produce particular patterns of results (in this case growth related). The best managers are systems thinkers. For example, they recognize that you cannot change one tire without checking the other three. Nor can you change the; brakes, suspension, gear ratios, engine, or just about anything else, without considering the knock-on implications. The same applies to business writers and consultants who tend to specialize on one particular area; leadership, talent, strategy or customer acquisition & retention. It also applies to organizations that are divided into functional silos ranging from HR, to Finance and Marketing. Just like a sophisticated racing machine, a Revenue Generating / Value Creating Machine needs a team of mechanics and a full toolbox if it is to perform to the max.

...strategy is an iterative process in which all of the moving parts influence one another and must be taken into account together.
A.G. Lafley & Roger L. Martin[113]

FORMULA BEATS STRATEGY

Everybody has their own definition of strategy - what it is and what it isn't, whose job it is and so on. But regardless of what you think about strategy and whether you think one is needed or not, you do need a formula for your organization, business unit, or team's growth. That means addressing all those factors that will help your organization to accelerate growth and thereby to win. It also means attending to the factors that can slow your organization down.

Strategy = **Formula** for Growth™

We prefer to say you need a formula for growth rather than a strategy for growth. That is because you are going to require:

- A focus on sustained profitable growth, rather than just sales

- A definition of growth that enables your team and organization to win, as well as its customers and partners

- Greater organizational buy-in and effective cross-functional collaboration

- An agile / adaptive approach that will enable you to adjust to changing market conditions as and when required.

The Formula for Growth™ reframes the debate about business performance to bypass the debate about; what strategy is / is not, who creates it, who owns it and most of all how it is to be executed.

In Section 6 (the Pitstop) we will examine some of the limitations of the traditional approach to strategy and the need to blend; strategy with execution, running the numbers with creative problem solving and bottom-up involvement with top down control.

An Updated Mental Model

To effect change on the most fundamental level you must change people's interpretation of reality – how they see a particular situation and their relationship to it. That is their mental model. The Formula for Growth™ has been designed to engage and indeed challenge the attitudes and beliefs that shape the behaviors, as well as the strategies of managers and their teams. It works to change the dominant mental models relating to performance and growth within your business to reflect your organization's growth needs / aspirations.

> In a world of deep complexity and extensive information the work of making sense has never been harder - or more important.
> Yoram Wind and Colin Crooke[114]

> Time to approach strategy in a different way and time to transform the process from a mechanical, analytical activity to something deeper, more meaningful, and far more rewarding for a leader.
> Cynthia Montgomery[115]

WHAT'S YOUR FORMULA?

Of course there isn't just one formula for growth™. Each company is different, so while the primary ingredients are the same across industries markets and continents, the precise formulation will be unique to your company at a particular point in time. With this in mind; what is your Formula for Growth™? What are the key ingredients for accelerated growth of your organization, business unit, or team at this time?

> '...to make the most of your limited time and money by focusing your efforts on the aspects of race car tuning and driving that matter the most'.
> Neil Roberts[116]

The labels used for the different parts of the Formula for Growth™ have been carefully chosen in order to be as widely applicable as possible, for example they are chosen to travel well, in terms of different geographies, industries and languages. Moreover, they are designed to minimize (as much as is possible) any issues of contention or misinterpretation. That said the labels are totally flexible – you can tailor them to your business and industry as required. So, go ahead and adjust any of the labels around the car or team that you feel would best fit your business.

Answers:

Here are the answers to the 'Modelling Performance' quiz on page 74.

1 Aligning Sales & Strategy Model (Frank Cespedes)
6 Business Canvass (Ostewalder & Pigneur)
2 Playing to Win Model (Lafley & Martin)
4 Diamond Model by Don Hambrick & Jim Fredrickson
3 Porter's 5 Forces Model
5 Mc Kinsey's 7 Ss

SUMMARY

The summary of this section is a visual one – the Formula for Growth™.

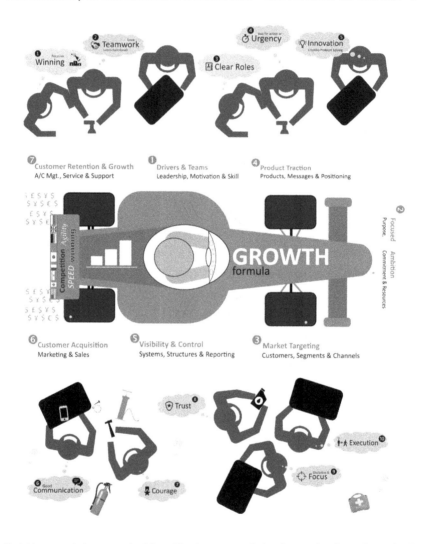

Put the model to work: Identify the part of the formula that if worked upon would most boost your success, or accelerate growth.

Part 2:

THE SPEED TESTS

SECTION 5

GROWTH MACHINE

*I'm a car fanatic and each morning I wake up
with a smile on my face...*
Murray Walker[117]

INTRODUCTION

Your organization is a revenue generating / value creating machine - that is its ultimate purpose. But has it been engineered to deliver sustained and profitable growth? In this section we explore the mechanics of accelerating your growth strategy and its execution. But we will start with a physics lesson.

Some people mistakenly think Formula One™ racing is just about speed. 'Acceleration 101' – an introductory class on physics of going faster – makes clear that accelerating isn't just about speed, but about direction/velocity too. The difference between the two is useful in exploring the Formula for Growth™. It also explains why some managers are more concerned with the back of the car than the front of the car.

ACCELERATION PRINCIPLE 1:

Accelerating isn't just about speed, but velocity.

Yes, speed is important, but unless you are going in a straight line, it is not the only factor. After all there is no point in accelerating in the wrong direction – where the car is pointed is a key factor too.

> *Moving in a straight line can be dangerous; somewhere you are going to hit something. Twisting and turning while moving around.... this is the adaptive part of strategizing.*
> Kees van der Heijden[118]

Velocity is about direction, as well as speed. It measures 'speed in a specific direction' *versus* speed in any direction.

Speed x Direction = Velocity. This is an important equation for any manager or leader concerned with accelerating growth. It is the equation for profitable and sustainable growth. After all there is no point in accelerating in the wrong (strategic) direction.

Velocity is:

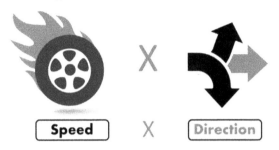

Any manager who has experience of a poorly-targeted marketing or sales campaign that doesn't quite hit the mark knows all too well the importance of strategic direction. However, in the race to meet end-of-quarter or end-of-year targets, precision often gets sacrificed for speed. But going off course by just a degree at the start can take you miles away from your desired finishing point over time.

> Speed refers to 'how fast an object is moving.' It does not care about direction. Velocity on the other hand refers to 'the rate at which an object changes its position.' Velocity is direction-aware. Acceleration then measures a change in velocity.
> The Physics Hypertextbook[119]

Understanding that acceleration means velocity and not just speed leads to two questions:

- The **speed** question: Are we going fast enough?
- The **direction** question: Are we heading in the right direction?

Both questions must be answered in tandem though, advocates of strategy argue that the latter question is the most important. Where the organization directs its efforts and resources is key; in particular, the choice of products, customers and markets is a major determinant of margins and profitability. Too many managers are focused on speed, but don't pay enough attention to direction.

> *When the external circumstances are so challenging that your current way of doing business cannot be sustained, decisively changing course is the only way to not only survive, but also to secure another chance to thrive.*
> Martin Reeves, Knut Haanaes & Janmejaya Sinha[120]

F1™ racing cars go incredibly fast. However, they are only at full throttle for just over half of the time that the car is racing. Circuits have lots of twists and turns. A key factor limiting the speed of the car is the requirement to maintain traction with the road when turning sharp corners. That is why accelerating is not just about speed.

> *... no object has ever travelled in a straight line with constant acceleration anywhere in the universe at any time — not today, not yesterday, not tomorrow, not five billion years ago, not thirty billion years in the future, never. This I can say with absolute metaphysical certainty.*
> The Physics Hypertextbook[121]

ACCELERATION PRINCIPLE 2:

Accelerating is about the rate of change in velocity over time.

Acceleration doesn't just mean going fast. It means going **faster**. It measures the rate of change in an organization's speed as well as its direction.

Acceleration is:

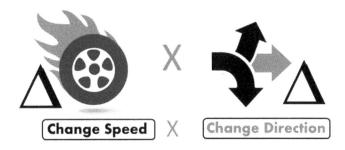

Change Speed X **Change Direction**

Acceleration is relative rather than absolute. It is measured not at a single point, but over time, which introduces an element of sustainability into the equation.

Sustainability is important because the speed and direction of your organization (its growth velocity) will have to change this year, next year and again the year after if it is to keep pace with the exponential rate of change in your external environment. So whatever speed you are going at today, it needs to be faster tomorrow. Moreover, be prepared that the direction will need to be adjusted on an ongoing basis too.

It's about accelerating change

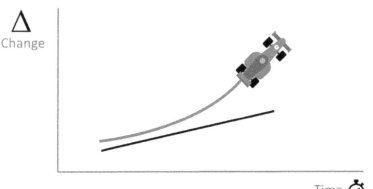

APPLYING PHYSICS TO THE FORMULA

The Speed by Direction equation has direct relevance to accelerating any machine and in particular your revenue generating/value creating machine. To explore this further let's break the machine down into three parts.

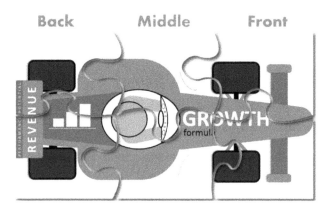

The **back** of the machine is the speed part of the velocity equation. It provides the power or speed. For an organization it is the power to acquire and retain customers. F1™ cars are rear-wheel drive with the engine or propulsion / power unit located behind the driver.

The **front** of the machine – in particular the nose cone and the front wheels – provides the direction. This is the direction part of the velocity equation, or the direction-setting role of strategy in setting out what the organization or business unit wants to achieve and the product-markets it aims to serve.

In the **middle** of the machine is the driver and the controls – the dashboard, clutch, throttle and so on. This is where the power from the back and the direction at the front should be managed. Here is a mix of hard and soft – where the passion and skill of the driver meets the plans, processes, systems and structures of the organization.

The front of your revenue generating / value creating machine sets direction – the direction-setting variables of strategy include what we sell and who we sell to, or where we compete and how we win. The engine at the back of the car executes on the strategy – it delivers traction and forward momentum. However, both parts of the car (front and back) must be in alignment. The same is true in any organization. For example, there is no point in accelerating growth into markets where the organization cannot ultimately win (in terms of profitable customers and sales). When it comes to growth a balance of power and precision is essential.

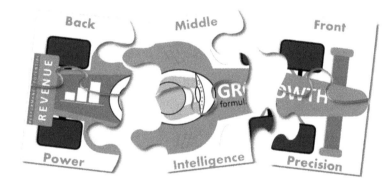

One manager in a Dubai Growth Pitstop™ workshop labelled the three parts of the car as follows:

- The road ahead.
- The power behind.
- The driver in the middle.

What part of the car is the key priority for your organization at this time? Is it the front, the middle or the back? Before you answer consider that, when it comes to fast cars and fast organizations, there are two different types of engineers / managers: those concerned with the back of the car and those concerned with the front of the car – what we have labelled the Enzo Ferrari and Colin Chapman archetypes.

	Enzo Ferrari	Colin Chapman
Founded:	Scuderia Ferrari F1™	Lotus F1™
Training:	Carpenter and Racer	Engineer and Pilot
Focused on:	Back of car	Front of car
Obsessed with:	Engine power	Aerodynamics, Lightness and Precision

In the 1960s Formula One™ racing was about speed and little else. The following quote by Ferrari's founder is representative of the time:

Enzo Ferrari famously said:

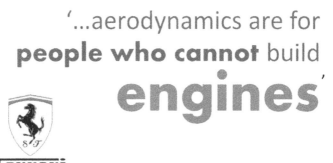

'...aerodynamics are for **people who cannot** build **engines**'

Enzo Ferrari even designed a racing car that had two engines – front and back. Although capable of reaching great speeds, the car simply did not have good enough handling to be successful on the racetrack[122]. A car that is all engine and little else won't work!

Enzo Ferrari's engine obsession dates from a time before the importance of car aerodynamics was fully understood. Furthermore, in modern racing, engine size and power is standardized across all teams. There are even requirements in terms of fuel efficiency. That means teams must look for performance advantages beyond the engine.

Going fast requires more than a big engine. That was the view of Colin Chapman founder of Lotus and a pioneering force for technical innovation in F1™ in the 1960s and 1970s.

A pilot and engineer, Chapman is largely responsible for the shape of the modern F1™ racing car, including the pointed nose cone (with radiators either side of the car rather than at the front) and other aerodynamic features. For him the focus was on precision at the front and not just power at the back.

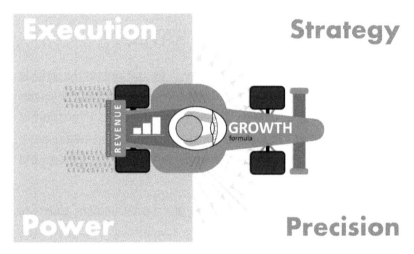

Listen to any Formula One™ champion and they will tell you that winning is about precision, as much as speed. The parallels with strategies for growth are real.

> *It is not bravery going at full speed, it is technical precision.*
> Jean-Pierre Beltoise[123]

The same principles apply in accelerating growth. The precision with which your company directs its products and services, as well as its sales and marketing efforts and resources, determines the growth rate it will enjoy.

Strategy is the result of choices executives make, on where to play and how to win, to maximize long-term value.
Ken Favaro *et al*[124]

Put simply, some customers, market segments and channels have the potential to generate faster and more profitable growth than others. Targeting those most profitable growth opportunities is key.

HOW PRECISE IS YOUR STRATEGY?

Having a powerful well-maintained engine is no use unless the vehicle can accelerate in the right direction. The power or capacity of the sales and marketing engine to deliver the growth required is a function of how precisely targeted the strategies, campaigns and messages are – measured in terms of the degree of traction in the chosen markets and segments.

Being strategic means making the core directional choices that will best maximize competitive success. More specifically it is about the choice of markets (or market segments) and products (or positioning). These directional choices are key to accelerating sustained profitable growth. For this reason, you could replace the word 'precision' with the word 'profit' in talking about the front of the car (revenue generating / value creating machine).

The front of the racing car looks a lot like an arrow-head (as in the diagram). It needs to be pointed at the customers you are chasing and the competitors you are overtaking. It is all about the markets you are accelerating into, or out of.

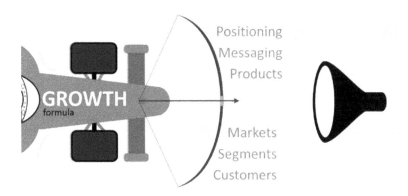

Positioning
Messaging
Products

Markets
Segments
Customers

Q: If your company wanted to accelerate growth where would you direct its activities? What customers, markets and channels would you prioritize? Would you steer clear of certain customers and segments if you wanted to ensure your success?

If you are going for growth, then you must steer your efforts with greater precision in the direction of those customers and channels that offer the greatest potential for growth. That means you need the Colin Chapman mentality – working on the front of the car. The rewards can be great – the successful positioning (or repositioning) of your company in a new and more profitable niche can be a major driver of revenue and margin.

If your company is already targeting in a precise manner the most attractive and most amenable markets and segments, then you may need an Enzo Ferrari mentality, to help build your sales and marketing engine so that it can generate more leads, enquires, clicks, etc. and convert them into revenue.

> *...consider the real work of strategy as beginning with where to play and how to win – the very heart of strategy. These are the choices that actually define what you will do, and where you will do it, so as to generate competitive advantage.*
> A.G. Lafley & Roger L. Martin[125]

THE PERFECT BALANCE

To build the ultimate racing car a combination of Chapman and Ferrari approaches would be a winning formula. It would apply engineering genius to both the back and the front of the car – the balance of both power and precision. Such a balance in your organization is essential too. There are five reasons why:

1. There is no point **accelerating in the wrong direction**. The choice of customers and segments is fundamental to winning.

2. The **front wheels of the car must be in alignment** if the car is to perform to its full potential. Ensuring the optimal fit between products / messages and customers / markets is key.

Balanced...

3. There is **no point perfecting the steering**, the front wheels or the aerodynamics of the nose cone if the engine is underpowered. Strategies (even winning ones) often fail at the point of execution.

4. There is **no point in building a more powerful engine** if going faster only results in increased noise and vibration coming from the front of the car. Most problems at the back of the car derive from problems at the front – most sales problems are really strategy problems.

5. You can't have **two sets of engineers** working on the front and back of the car that don't talk to each other. The alignment of sales and service (back of car) and product marketing (front of car) is key to sustaining profitable growth. You might as well just saw the car in half!

Achieving a balance between front and rear is not easy, however. Most high-performance cars are rear-wheel drive, with the power coming from the rear wheels. Anybody who has ever driven a rear-wheel drive car knows that extra care is needed on a slippery winding road (like those found in so many markets). The greater weight at the back of the car, combined with the fast-spinning back wheels, can easily result in a situation where the nose of the car goes in one direction and the back of the car in another. This problem is commonly experienced in organizations seeking to accelerate growth.

A CAR SAWED IN HALF

Do you have two halves or one full car? The artificial distinction between strategy and execution, or between sales and marketing, is the equivalent of sawing the car in half. Yet it is very prevalent.

Traditionally the greatness of a strategy was measured in terms of its ambition and vision. Strategies were highly aspirational – they were about vision, mission and purpose. But what good is aspirations and visions unless they are translated into reality. Management sets out a wonderful strategy - they imagine the car heading in a new exciting direction, but nobody actually takes the steering wheel and makes it happen. It is the classic gap between strategy and implementation and the number one reason why strategies fail.

> *The strategy journey to success is long and dangerous. Most strategies lose between 40 and 60 percent of their financial potential along the execution highway.*
> Jeroen De Flander[126]

A central theme of this book is that strategy and execution, as well as marketing, sales and operations, must be seamlessly interconnected. The back of the car cannot work in isolation of the front. If there are problems with the front of the car they will impact on the back and *vice versa*.

Our research and our experience have convinced us that growth and profit are ultimately the result of alignment between people, customers, strategy, and processes.
George Labovitz & Victor Rosansky[127]

One manager in a Nordics pitstop explained the duality in his organization like this:

The sales team is at the back revving the engine like crazy... The marketing people are at the front adjusting messaging, targeting and so on. Occasionally they shout at each other but the noise of the engine makes any real communication between the two difficult.
Manager – Pharmaceuticals

As Frank Cespedes, one of Harvard's leading experts, points out in a recent book many so-called 'sales problems' are really 'strategic alignment issues.'[128] Welding the two parts of the car together is vital. The requirements of growth trump the politics of any individual function – both must share one clear unifying goal – making the car go faster.

The most crucial connection in an organization seeking to grow is between sales and strategy. But if your company is like most, instead of linkage there is a widening gap... It's time to address the enormous cost of the strategy-sales gap.
Frank V. Cespedes[129]

THE PIVOT POINT

The growth trajectory of an organization or business unit is a complex equation. That is because direction is set at 3 different points. Just a few degrees out of alignment at any of these areas and the trajectory of the car or organization gets confused. It looks crazy when you see what this would look like for a racing car (see diagram), but this is effectively what happens in many organizations.

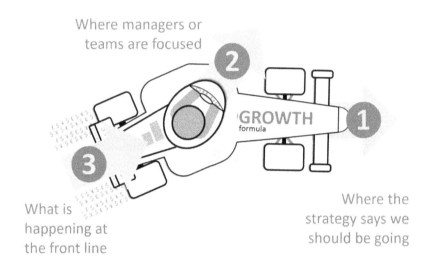

Where managers or teams are focused

Where the strategy says we should be going

What is happening at the front line

Engines know or care little of direction. They do what engines do – burn fuel to create power that the driver can then transfer to the wheels in a controlled manner (*via* the throttle, clutch and brakes). The important part of racing is what the driver does with the power – the same is true in business.

The driver (sometimes called the pilot) has a key role to play in steering the car where is needs to go. He/she has to adjust the steering continually to ensure that all aspects of the car are in alignment. His or her job is to ensure that what is set out in the strategy (front of car) and what is happening at the front line/in the marketplace are in alignment. That requires continual adjustment. What is crucially important however is where the manager is focused. If managers are not focused on what is in the strategy or what is happening in terms of its implementation, then the car will naturally go out of alignment.

If the front of the car is measured in terms of precision and the back of the car in terms of power, then the middle of the car is measured in terms of intelligence and skill. Here is where choices are made in terms of products and markets, as well as the fit between the external environment and the allocation of the company's efforts and resources.

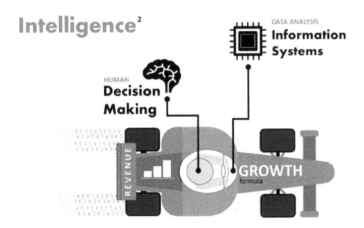

Perfect alignment is a measure of the intelligence, sophistication and responsiveness of Sales, Marketing, Operations, Customer Services and Finance.

In Formula 1™ there is precision in every turn – the driver instinctively knows when to brake on approaching a corner and when to accelerate out of a corner. The performance of the car depends on the ability of driver to take the car to the maximum speed consistent with the tires retaining traction with the road. If you lose traction then speed is futile, even dangerous. Buckled tightly into their seat and so close to the ground – the driver has a real feel for the road and how the car is handling. Moreover, a racing car driver also has information systems that feedback instantly to him and to the rest of the team on the level of speed, traction and general performance of both the engine and the car. That information enables the driver to make good decisions. The pity is that most managers cannot look at a dashboard to see how they are performing.

> *Q: In your race to accelerate which do you need most: more power or greater precision?*

WHAT IS YOUR FOCUS?

In many organizations there is a tension between power and precision – a tension that is intensified by the pressure to meet targets in the race to the end of the quarter or end of the year. But there must be time for precision even in the midst of the most frantic quarter-end or year-end, because as a racing driver might say: "You cannot always have your foot on the throttle." So where will you focus to accelerate growth? Are you like Enzo Ferrari (focused on speed and in particular a more powerful engine), or Colin Chapman (focused on aerodynamics, traction and precision)? Perhaps you are committed to investing equally in both?

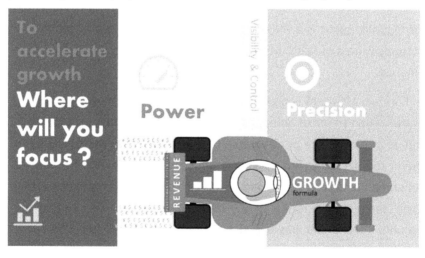

> *Q: If your organization does not achieve its full growth potential will it because of a lack of power or a lack of precision?*

The close fit between strategy (which is typically seen as "what business to pursue") and execution ("how to pursue and sustain it") is ingrained in every decision that people in your company make.

Paul Leinwand & Cesare R. Mainardi[130]

In Growth Pitstop™ workshops some people pick the front of the car, others the back and more the middle - as shown in the photo here. Then team members set to work on their chosen part of the Formula for Growth™. They define the area as it is today and set a goal for improvement, together with an expected impact on growth. Then they identify what the organization needs to do, as well as what they themselves need to do.

Rather than trying to fix everything at once it is a good idea to focus on one or just a few areas of your Revenue Generating/Value Creating Machine to work on at a particular time. So just like a pitlane mechanic work first on the parts of the car that are most important. That is the parts of the machine that are slowing you down, or have the most potential (if addressed) to accelerate growth.

What part of the revenue generating/value creating machine, if worked upon, would most boost success, or accelerate growth?

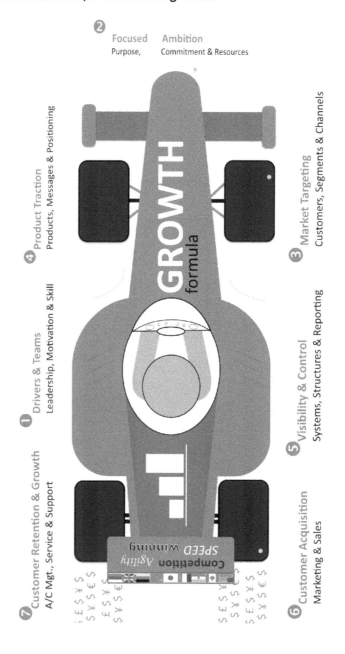

We would recommend picking parts of the formula that are within <u>your</u> control (or the control of your team) and that, if improved, would most boost <u>your</u> success. There may be parts of the formula that you want to fix, but the timing is just not right, or you don't have all the tools or resources that will be required.   So prioritize working on an area that you feel can confidently deliver benefits in the short to medium term.

When you have selected an area estimate the percentage impact that fixing it could have on the success of the business. By doing this you are answering the 'Why?' question and clarifying the motivation, as well as the justification, for working on the chosen aspect of your organization, business unit or team growth strategy.

The companion book, called Formula for Growth™ explores the mechanics of the Revenue Generating/Value Creating machine in more detail. Running to over 400 pages it integrates performance and global benchmarking data to examine each part of the car and how it can be optimized for peak performance. You will find more details in the appendix.

SUMMARY – THE GROWTH MACHINE

Acceleration doesn't just mean going fast. It means going faster. It measures the rate of change in an organization's speed as well as its direction. That is important in terms of your Revenue Generating/Value Creating Machine:

- The **back** of the machine provides the power or speed. For an organization it is the power to generate revenue and ultimately to acquire and retain customers.

- The **front** of the machine – in particular the nose cone and the front wheels – provides the direction. This is the direction-setting role of strategy - setting out what the organization or business unit wants to achieve and the product-markets it aims to serve.

- In the **middle** of the car is the driver and the controls – the dashboard, clutch, throttle and so on. Here is a mix of hard and soft – where the passion and skill of the driver meets the plans, processes, systems and structures of the organization.

The question is: *'What part of the revenue generating/value creating, if worked upon, would most boost your success, or accelerate growth?'*

Like most racing cars organizations are rear-wheel-drive, so be careful since power from the back depends on direction from the front. When it comes to growth a perfect balance between power (at the back) and precision (at the front) is essential. Alignment is key.

Section 6

PITSTOP

...it's paradoxical that one of the most important parts of a Grand Prix comes when the car is stationary.

Mark Gallagher[131]

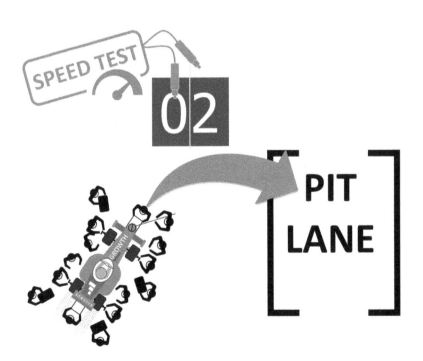

INTRODUCTION

For your organization the road ahead has many twists and turns - the result of fast changing technology, channels and customer needs. Because you can't always see what's around the bend, managers must be ready to adapt in an instant to any sudden surprises. They must be agile, as well as fast.

In this section we explore how winning in a faster and more competitive race requires a different style of driving and perhaps even a new type of vehicle (i.e. revenue generating/value creating machine). For leaders and their organizations, it requires not just a great growth strategy or plan, but the ability to adapt it at the first sign of an emerging opportunity or threat. In short it requires the ability to pitstop.

THE FASTEST OF TIMES

Every generation of leader and manager has read warnings about the pace of change. They have been admonished to embrace change and to 'thrive on chaos'[132]. But if some companies were struggling to cope in the 1980's and 90's then they are really going to struggle with today's accelerated pace of change - that is if they are still around!

> This is not an age of defensive castles, moats, and armour. It is rather an age of cunning, speed, and surprise.
> Richard D'Aveni (1994)[133]

An entire century worth of change - that is how futurologists describe what we have all experienced in the last two decades. But hold on tight your company is set to see as much as double that rate of change over the next decade[134]. Those are F1™ type speeds!

'...we won't experience 100 years of progress in the 21st century—it will be more like 20,000 years of progress (at today's rate)'.
Ray Kurzweil[135]

Markets Are Accelerating at F1™ Speeds

In a fast accelerating marketplace either an organization is keeping up, or falling behind. The question is which is accelerating faster: your industry or your organization.

Which is accelerating faster?

YOUR ORGANIZATION
(Internal Acceleration)

THE MARKET SPACE
(External Acceleration)

A problem happens when the rate of acceleration or change in an industry or market exceeds the rate within an organization or business unit. Yet this is happening in many organizations. According to Growth Pitstop™ benchmarking data managers score their organizations at just 63% in terms of their ability to predict and respond to market changes.

Slower moving companies can all too easily be overtaken by events in their markets. They struggle to adapt once successful strategies to new market realities - new technologies, new customer trends and most important of all - new competitors. The problem is that while markets are apt to change, many companies are not. For companies that were built in a stable environment, it can be a challenge to adjust to a dynamic fast changing one. An accelerating rate of change brings with it new complexity and uncertainty. It is no longer about straight-line acceleration.

> *...the percentage of companies falling out of the top three revenue rankings in their industry each year... was around 8 percent in 2013.*
> Martin Reeves, Knut Haanaes & Janmejaya Sinha[136]

A NEW BASIS OF COMPETITION

For most industries the road ahead has many twists and turns – the result of fast changing customers, competitors and channels. As in F1™ these sharp corners make agility as important as speed.

The Road Ahead has many Twists & Turns

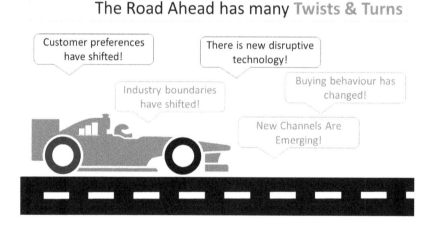

A F1™ race track can have as many as 17 corners over the course of a 3.3km circuit! That compares to the much more straight-forward oval circuit used in NASCAR™ racing for example. These two types of circuits are a metaphor for the nature of the industries in which organizations compete and the different demands that they place on drivers/leaders and their cars/strategies.

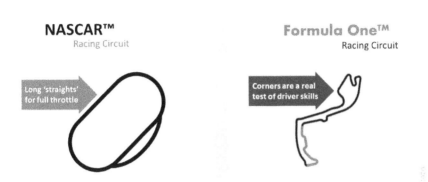

For most managers the track upon which they compete has changed significantly and will continue to change. Most industries, indeed most of the world of modern commerce, is in a NASCAR™- to F1™- like progression. That is to say it has got faster, more competitive and more complex. This places new demands on the machinery of business requiring greater speed, agility, skill, teamwork and innovation.

> *Straight roads are for fast cars, turns are for fast drivers.*
> Colin McRae[137]

VUCA REQUIRES F1™-LIKE ABILITIES

Few today would argue that the rate of change is faster than at any time in the past. Customer needs shift, new segments appear, and new competitors emerge at an accelerated pace. New market opportunities appear, transform and disappear faster than ever. This accelerating rate of change results in an increasingly complex business environment – one that is well described by the term VUCA.

> *Change is multifaceted, relentless, seditious, and occasionally shocking. In this maelstrom, long-lived political dynasties, venerable institutions, and hundred-year-old business models are all at risk.*
> Garry Hammel[138]

Originally used by military planners, VUCA is a phrase that has gained popularity among business leaders grappling with change. It is a metaphor for the zigzag race circuit, with blind corners, tight turns and awkwardly-placed chicanes that require F1™ - like levels of speed, agility and innovation.

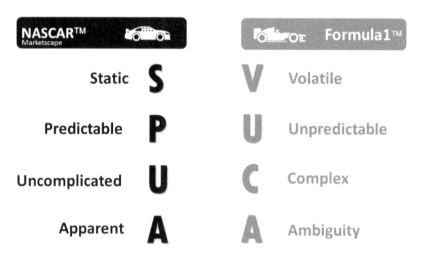

Unexpected changes are not bugs in the world's operating system; they are a feature.
Donald Sull[139]

The opposite of VUCA is a market that is stable, predictable, uncomplicated and apparent – SPUA, which is akin to the oval circuit in NASCAR™. It is a competitive racing duel and there are crashes, but unlike F1™ the car can be at full throttle for much of the race. The NASCAR™- style track with its long straights and oval shape reflects an industry and even a way of doing business that is more predictable and more manageable. By contrast the twists and turns of the F1™ circuit make it the most complex and demanding motor sport, as well as a powerful metaphor for a more complex, demanding and unpredictable industry landscape – one that requires more sophisticated strategies and skilled drivers, as well as greater innovation and agility.

> Today four out of five CEOs expect a major change in their industry over the short to medium term.
> IBM[140]

PROFILE YOUR INDUSTRY  EXERCISE

Are you living in a SPUA or VUCA world? Using the scale provided indicate the degree to which the statements on the left or the right best describe the marketspace in which you compete.

SPUA		VUCA
Stable – There is little change in the market space in terms of competition, customers, channels, technology, etc.	1 2 3 4 5	**Volatile** – The market is dynamic and fast moving. New market opportunities and challenges continually emerge, transform and disappear.
Predictable – It is easy to foretell changes in the marketplace, such as technology, and competition.	1 2 3 4 5	**Uncertain** – Accurately predicting the future is difficult or impossible. Be prepared for surprises!
Uncomplicated – Business strategies, technologies and solutions are straightforward and relatively low risk.	1 2 3 4 5	**Complex** – The multiplicity of factors involved can cause confusion. There is no simple, or single, solution / strategy.
Apparent – Understanding what is happening in the market is easy and good information is readily available.	1 2 3 4 5	**Ambiguous** – A haziness makes it easy to misinterpret things. Don't expect to have full information before taking action.

> 'If you don't like change you are going to like irrelevance even less'
> Tom Peters[141]

Our world is increasingly more Volatile, Uncertain, Complex and Ambiguous. We need to turn VUCA into Vision, Understanding, Clarity and Agility if we are to succeed...
Jayne May & Charles May[142]

Calculating Your VUCA Score:

15-20: High VUCA: You are racing on the most demanding of circuits, with lots of surprises in store. Not only is the pace quickening but the rules are changing too with blurring industry boundaries, new channels and a shifting basis of competition. You will need a great car (plan or strategy), but also great agility – working to continually develop and refine the approach over time. You also need track-side feedback and the most skilled and responsive of drivers.

10-14: Increasing VUCA: There are signs of accelerated change and complexity in your industry. You will need to anticipate what is around the corner and innovate to keep ahead of the pack. You must seek out unmet customer needs and under-served customer segments. This is likely to require some test laps, innovation and experimentation.

5-9: Future VUCA: Avoid complacency and be ready to embrace future complexity and change. Indeed, look for pockets of opportunity in segments of customers with unmet needs, competitor weaknesses, new technologies or trends in parallel industries.

1-4: VUCA FREE: Your industry (as you see it) is pretty straight-forward and uncomplicated. The pace of change and innovation is low. However, this may mean that profitability and growth are in decline due to industry maturity. If so, the real opportunities to accelerate growth may be elsewhere.

If everything seems under control, you're just not going fast enough.
Mario Andretti[143]

Tip: Some people may be more sensitive to the rate of change in your industry than others. So, ask a number of people to complete the VUCA scale. Getting a number of different perspectives is important to generating a dialog on the basis for winning in your industry today, as well as tomorrow.

> *'Volatility in revenue growth, in revenue ranking and in operating margins have all more than doubled since the 1960s'.*
> Reeves, Love & Mathur[144]

ARE YOU VUCA OR F1™ READY?

Your organization may be successful in NASCAR™, but for those parts of your business where the competition is most aggressive and the market is most challenging, you need the speed and agility of a F1™ car.

> *It is a rule that you cannot make fortunes out of situations of certainty; market forces make sure that the returns are low if everybody can take equal advantage of the same opportunity... It is only in situations of uncertainty that opportunity for significant gain arises.*
> Ronald Cohen[145]

VUCA industries can present the greatest opportunities. That is unless you are put out by the old patterns being interrupted, the rules being re-written, or the status quo being disturbed. Fast changing markets often entail; new rules, a new urgency and a new basis of competition. They are characterised by blurring industry boundaries, morphing customer needs, the reinvention of business models and the emergence of new channels. These are fuelled by leaps of technology, social shifts and global economic volatility. All this can be scary at first, but then exhilarating. That is if you are racing the right type of car (AKA revenue generating machine) – one that combines agility with speed.

...firms that successfully match their strategy to their environment realized significantly better returns—4 to 8 percent of total shareholder return—over firms that didn't. Yet around half of all companies we looked at mismatch their approach to strategy to their environment in some way.
Martin Reeves, Knut Haanaes & Janmejaya Sinha[146]

Performing 'To the Limit'

The twists and turns on the F1™ racetrack require a pattern of rapid acceleration and sudden breaking that puts incredible pressure on the F1™ car's mechanical parts. Disk brakes and engine parts for example become white hot and tires reach pizza oven temperatures. It also puts great physical and mental pressure on the driver. F1™ is the very definition of what it means to perform at the limit. The limit of technology, biology and physics:

- Physics – Gravity would dictate that a car hurtling at high speed around a 90 degree (or sharper corner) should simply fly off into the air. But in F1™ that rarely happens.

- Technology – A F1™ race car is part car and part airplane. It has a nose cone and wings in order to cut through the air with maximum ease, as well as to generate the massive downforce that enables the car to stay on the road.

- Biology – Taking corners at high speed generates near black-out G forces for the driver. It takes incredible stamina and fitness to race in F1™.

To enable the driver and the machine to perform at the limit requires regular pitstops. These involve the essential maintenance required to keep the car in the race and to adapt to changing conditions.

'By the time 10 years has passed only one in three (organizations) will resemble what it looks like today'.
Chris Zook[147]

TWO MODES OF RESPONSE

If your organization is competing in an environment that is high on the VUCA scale its approach to strategy and execution should be different to that applied if it is low. You still need a plan to win. But predicting the future in a VUCA marketplace is no easy matter and the best laid plans are often laid to waste. So beware of traditional management strategies and techniques that were designed for steady and predicable SPUA markets (NASCAR™), not for dynamic and unpredictable VUCA markets (F1™). Nowhere is this clearer than in respect of strategy and execution.

> *The time-tested, comfortable approaches to everyday management don't work well in dynamic, rapidly changing, and therefore cruelly uncertain environments.*
> Rita Gunther McGrath & Ian C. Macmillan[148]

Strategy has a 'bad rap' with so many books on the subject pointing out its failings in the context of a complex and fast changing marketplace. Often repeated is the statistic which suggests that as many as 9 out of 10 strategies fail[149]. But of course these figures relate to the now mostly defunct traditional approach, or what we call SPUA Strategy. The modern approach to accelerating growth strategy – call it VUCA strategy – couldn't be more different. That is clear from the table overleaf.

The difference between the SPUA and VUCA approach to strategy can be summed up in one word: Pitstops. The latter is fast while the former has traditionally being slow - not just to devise, but also to implement, review and update. For example, strategy was traditionally set in a 2-3 year cycle, while a pitstop is scheduled several times during every race.

> *...increasing fast changing markets are not the problem, but rather the layers of complexity organizations have put in place to deal with it.*
> Yves Morieux and Peter Tollman[150]

Table: SPUA V's VUCA Strategy

	SPUA Strategy	VUCA Strategy
Fast	No	Yes
Agile/Dynamic	No	Yes
Bias for action	No	Yes
Hands on	No	Yes
Collaborative	No	Yes
Passion-fueled	No	Yes
Continuous Review	No	Yes

> *If the future is 100% uncertain planning is obviously a waste of time. The primary task therefore is to separate what is predictable from what is fundamentally uncertain.*
> Kees van der Heijden[151]

The traditional mode of business planning, performance management and strategy is fine for times where change is predictable and slow. Not surprisingly however it struggles to cope in the modern era where organizations must keep pace with an accelerating rate of change and uncertainty. Spotting a change too late, or responding to it too slowly means that an organization risks being overtaken by faster and nimbler competitors. Falling behind is easy, so too is falling so far back that you won't ever get to catch up, as happened to; Blockbuster, Polaroid and Nokia for example.

> *With speed low enough and predictability high enough, certain methods work just fine in organizations. But these methods cannot possibly work when speed goes up significantly and predictability (predictably) goes down. It becomes a different game.*
> John P. Kotter[152]

TRADITIONAL APPROACHES KILL AGILITY

Once a strategy is created the clock is ticking. It can suddenly be overtaken by a competitor, or enter into a skid due to changing track conditions. That means you have to be prepared to pull your strategy, plans, projects and initiatives into the pit lane at any time. Traditionally this didn't happen however. Indeed, if race teams approached performance management and strategy the way many organizations do:

1. Pitstops would only happen **sporadically** – often at the end of the race, or at least too late in the race for it to have any real impact on the outcome.

2. The race strategy set out prior to the race would be **adhered to rigidly** in spite of changing track conditions, the emerging strategies of competitors, or the feedback of the driver.

3. There would be committees rather than pit crews, with a lot more talk than action in the pitlane. Some of the **pit crew would be missing** and people would be working away on their own part of the car with little coordination or cross-functional collaboration.

4. The array of monitors that **data analysts** use to review data from the car would largely be blank, or populated with historic data rather than real time insights.

5. Pitstops would be a more relaxed affair – the sense of **urgency** would disappear – some teams might take up to a half an hour to get the car back in the race.

6. Drivers would be continually **giving out** about their cars, blaming the engineers and mechanics and failing to take responsibility for inputting to the design or maintenance of the car.

If race teams devised their strategies or reviewed their performance the way that most organizations have traditionally done the driver would probably decide not to pull into the pit lane because it wouldn't increase his, or her **chances of winning**. As a result, cars would be sliding on bald tires, skidding on wet tracks and retiring due to mechanical failure. On the winner's podium would be the driver with the good pit crew and the effective pitstops.

> *...strategy is now less about anticipating how the world will change, which is increasingly difficult to know, than about superiority at rapid testing, learning, changing, and adapting.*
> Chris Zook and James Allen[153]

If race teams stuck rigidly to their strategies, the way organizations have done, they couldn't win. It is not always possible to see what is around the corner, to predict the moves of a competitor, changes in track conditions, and so on. That means teams have to be ready to adapt in an instant. They start the race with a strategy, but if conditions change they will revise, perhaps even scrapping it, if it is no longer working.

> *Unless the culture promotes adaptability, where you are actively preparing for future transitions and shifts, your business success is entirely contingent on the current technology or product curve it is following.*
> Charles O'Reilly & Michael Tushman[154]

Dead or Just Dead Slow?

Strategy was declared dead way back in the early 1990's by Henry Mintzberg[155]. But maybe the problem isn't that strategy is dead, but rather that it is dead slow - slow to devise, slow to implement and slow to adjust. You need a plan, or strategy as much, if not more, today than you did two decades ago. But in a turbulent and fast changing world you don't just need a clever strategy, you need one that is fast and agile too.

Business planning is still rooted in an annual cycle of targets and budget setting that is indistinguishable from the centralized planning system of soviet Russia under Stalin.
Patrick Hoverstadt[156]

DYNAMIC APPROACHES ADD AGILITY

Most managers and organizations are already on a path of transition to a VUCA-ready strategy, rating their organization's approach to planning, strategy and execution at 64% according to the Growth Pitstop™ benchmarking data. They are increasingly managing performance the way race teams do. That includes:

1. Setting out with a clear plan or strategy, but being ready to quickly adjust it (or even scrap it) if it isn't working.

2. Putting the same emphasis on great execution as a clever strategy.

3. Being ready to respond with lightning speed to a change in market conditions, the moves of competitors and so on.

4. Continually monitoring what is working and what is not working in the relentless quest for the millisecond advantage.

5. Working effectively as a team – on a cross functional basis – with a single purpose in mind: to maximize the chances of winning.

The principles of a more dynamic and ultimately more effective approach to performance management and strategic execution are to be found in a pitstop. A race team would never start a race without a carefully considered strategy. That is a strategy to maximize the chances of winning by matching driver skill and vehicle performance to the competition and the condition of the track. However, the team is not slave to a strategy that is under-performing. They won't hesitate to pull the car into the pit lane in order to make any adjustments that are required in order to maximize success. That includes changing the tires, adjusting the nose cone, switching the controls (steering wheel) and so on. The means of adjusting and adapting the strategy in response to change is the pitstop. They are perhaps the most efficient of all plan-do-review cycles. The perfect blend of strategy and execution. They are about adjustment, calibration and optimization.

> *Adaptive environments require continuous experimentation because planning does not work under conditions of rapid change and unpredictability.*
> Martin Reeves, Knut Haanaes & Janmejaya Sinha[157]

PERFORMANCE OPTIMIZATION

VUCA and the pitstop are not just a matter of strategy and execution, but of the performance of plans, projects, programmes, and of course people. But while performance management is clearly on the management agenda, it is an area with which many struggle[158]. For example, here are some of the words that managers typically associate with performance management in their organizations – you will note that most of them are negative:

- Pressure
- Uncomfortable
- Dreaded
- Contentious

- Dispute
- Argument
- Review
- Evaluation

- Problems
- Non-performers
- Success
- Plan

How performance is managed in F1™ - in particular the role of the pitstop - offers inspiration for managers and their teams. Use the checklist overleaf to identify how your organization could improve its approach to performance management (PM).

 **EXERCISE**

Tick any of the following that are opportunities for improvement:

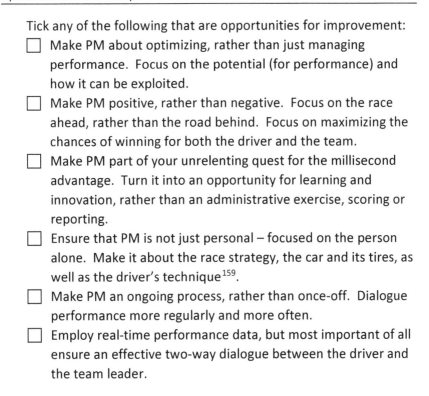

- ☐ Make PM about optimizing, rather than just managing performance. Focus on the potential (for performance) and how it can be exploited.
- ☐ Make PM positive, rather than negative. Focus on the race ahead, rather than the road behind. Focus on maximizing the chances of winning for both the driver and the team.
- ☐ Make PM part of your unrelenting quest for the millisecond advantage. Turn it into an opportunity for learning and innovation, rather than an administrative exercise, scoring or reporting.
- ☐ Ensure that PM is not just personal – focused on the person alone. Make it about the race strategy, the car and its tires, as well as the driver's technique[159].
- ☐ Make PM an ongoing process, rather than once-off. Dialogue performance more regularly and more often.
- ☐ Employ real-time performance data, but most important of all ensure an effective two-way dialogue between the driver and the team leader.

The pitstop takes place 'in the heat of the action' - at a time when it can have the maximum impact on the outcome. There is, after all, no point in reviewing performance after the race has been run. Yet that is what many organizations are prone to do. Take for example the often dreaded annual performance review. Taking place in twelve month intervals the annual performance review often takes the form of a post-mortem on the year that has passed. Moreover, the next conversation about performance may not take place for another 50 weeks!

> *We've arrived at a very different and much simpler design for managing people's performance. Its hallmarks are speed, agility, one-size-fits-one, and constant learning, and it's underpinned by a new way of collecting reliable performance data.*
> Marcus Buckingham & Ashley Goodall[160]

Pitstops V's Annual Reviews

Annual Performance Reviews have long come in for criticism, but now some of the world's biggest names, GE, Netflix and Accenture, have scrapped the ritual in favor of a more regular performance dialog and ongoing coaching behavior[161]. This approach is aimed at developing, rather than simply managing performance, and seeks to address employee needs for more frequent feedback, open communication and better collaboration with peers[162]. The pitstop is not a once-off intervention, but a system of ongoing support to the driver and the car. It is an unrelenting approach to performance management and behavioral change – it is not just once off, but ongoing.

> Agile approaches excel in volatile environments in which conformance to plans made months in advance is a poor measure of success. ...Traditional measures of success emphasize conformance to predictions (plans). Agility emphasizes responsiveness to change...
>
> Jim Highsmith[163]

ADAPTIVE PITSTOP BEHAVIOURS

A pitstop is important because you cannot always know what is around the corner, or what a competitor will do. It is difficult to predict how road conditions might change, or to anticipate a mechanical failure. The driver and the team have to be primed and ready to adapt, adjust or respond. They need to be agile - ready to pull the car into the pit lane as and when required. When this happens the team needs to be there ready to take action - to do whatever needs to be done to enable the car and the driver to maximize its chances of success. But it has to be fast - there isn't time for endless talking. For every minute that your car is out of the race, spectators (customers) are waiting and competitors are passing you by. The ability to adapt is an important source of competitive advantage – what we call the Pitstop Advantage.

> *From 2006 to 2011 companies ranked in the top decile in the BCG Adaptive Advantage Index grew their market capitalization by 31% more per year on average than the bottom decile companies.*
> Reeves, Love & Mathur[164]

Just like a pitstop VUCA strategy requires adaptive, behaviours and skills. In particular, there are seven characteristics of adaptive decision makers/making. Let's examine them now:

1. Imagination and creativity are as important as running the numbers, or doing the analysis. Historical precedents are of little value, indeed the requirement is to break free of the past, including old assumptions and beliefs. New solutions and strategies require **fresh thinking and creative problem solving**.

    > *...many, if not most, of the challenges you face today and will face tomorrow require something more than incorporating new technical skills... These are 'adaptive challenges' and they can only be met by transforming your mindset...*
    > Robert Kegan & Lisa Laskow Lahey[165]

2. Because there is no single 'right or wrong answer' a logical analytical approach is unlikely to be sufficient. Greater **creativity, experimentation and innovation** is required. That means more test laps, more experimentation and greater innovation.

    > *... in a world of change and flux, "more of the same" is rarely the right answer. ...one must have innovative or entrepreneurial component.*
    > Richard P. Rumelt[166]

3. Typically, one or few people cannot solve adaptive challenges, rather **multiple perspectives** are required. That means you need a

cross-functional pit team who will work trackside – close to the action.

> *...You must move quickly to an integrated growth organization and foster a culture that prioritizes growth across the company.*
> Sean Ellis & Morgan Brown[167]

4. The future is uncertain. Therefore, it is also important to engage **multiple alternative scenarios** before settling on a decision.

> *...the first objective of scenario-based planning became the generation of projects and decisions that are more robust under a variety of alternative futures.*
> Kees van der Heijden[168]

5. Being able to **roll-back on previous decisions** if they prove to be wrong, revise assumptions and to learn from mistakes.

> *A leader must be keen and alert to what drives a decision... If it was based on good logic... I felt comfortable in being unswerving ... Any other reason (or reasons) for persisting were examined carefully. Among the most common faulty reason are 1 trying to prove you are right and 2 trying to prove someone else is wrong.*
> Bill Walsh[169]

6. **Agile execution** is as important as a clever strategy definition. That means bringing those who develop and those who execute more closely together, giving more autonomy and freedom to manoeuvre to those on the track, as well as reviewing and revising not just the strategy but also the underlying process on a continual basis.

> *In an adaptive environment, winning comes from adapting to change by continuously experimenting and identifying new options more quickly and economically than others.*
> Reeves & Haanaes[170]

7. The leader's job is never done. Just as in F1™ there is a constant quest, both on and off the race track, for the millisecond advantage. It is about **continuous improvement and fast learning** – optimizing the car you have got, while working on an even better one for next year.

> *Too much business thinking implies a future state when the business will have "arrived"; more than just achieving stability, it will have reached a stage where the principal management challenge will be to keep it going. But this sort of stasis, even in a successful company, is illusory.*
> Rupert Merson[171]

How adaptive is your organization or team in its decision making? To find out take the test.

EXERCISE

7 Characteristics of Adaptive Decision Makers/Making	How your team scores *(Circle the scale below where 1= Very Poor, 5 = Very Good)*				
1 Fresh thinking	1	2	3	4	5
2 Experimentation & innovation	1	2	3	4	5
3 Engage multiple perspectives	1	2	3	4	5
4 Entertain alternative scenarios	1	2	3	4	5
5 Roll-back on previous decisions	1	2	3	4	5
6 Agile execution	1	2	3	4	5
7 Continuous improvement	1	2	3	4	5

What was your adaptiveness score? Find out what it means below:

High = 26 – 35: Your organization excels in terms of execution, innovation and fast learning. This represents a competitive advantage.

Medium = 16 – 25: There are likely to be others in your industry that can more speedily exploit emerging marketplace opportunities or threats. It is time to address the barriers to increased agility and a more adaptive approach to business strategy and execution.

Low = Less than 15: Warning. Your organization is at risk of being overtaken by the quickening pace of market change. It is not adapting or innovating fast enough. It is time to reinvent how your organization sets and reviews strategy. Change the locus of decision making, engage more collaboratively (especially from the front line) and create an environment that facilitates more open debate and a more balanced approach to risk taking and innovation.

> *Turbulence… has an upside… Seeing a turbulent world through threat-tinted glasses invites the dysfunctions of threat rigidity— centralized control, limited experimentation, and focus on existing resources—that stymies the pursuit of opportunity.*
> Donald Sull[172]

RE-THINKING STRATEGY

Much of what we traditionally have associated with strategy is unhelpful. That includes:

- Strategy = vision, mission or purpose (big picture aspiration not practical reality)

- Strategy = senior executive, strategist, or consultant (top down, as opposed to bottom up)

- Strategy = analysis, logic, clarity (as opposed to creativity, innovation, uncertainty)

- Strategy = answers (as opposed to questions)

- Strategy = knowing (as opposed to learning)

- Strategy = certainty (as opposed to curiosity & experimentation)

- Strategy = something you set slowly and stick to rigidly (as opposed to agile & dynamic)

- Strategy = planning (implementation = somebody else's job)

Formal planning processes with deadlines and pre-formatted reports are the enemy of thinking.
Kees van der Heijden[173]

Does your organization hold any of the above out-dated notions of strategy? Tick  the ones that reflect the way you and your team thinks. If you ticked more than 3, your organization's approach to strategy may be slowing you down.

The dilemma is: Do you throw traditional strategy away and begin again, or do you try to rehabilitate it? For example, keep the traditional approach to planning, the hierarchies, structures and controls that you have relied on for decades, but complement it with other more agile, creative and innovative approaches. Sure develop your mission statement, write the strategic plan - do all the things that your organization has always done around planning and strategy. But don't stop there! Form your pit team and engage more widely in reviewing your strategy, spend more time trackside, make more regular adjustments, do more test laps, gather more data, listen to your drivers, and most important of all bring passion to the fore by focusing on winning. All of these things are characteristics of the pitstop approach and are reflective of the type of dynamic strategy that wins today's races.

A new strategy is, in the language of science, a hypothesis, and its implementation is an experiment...
Richard P. Rumelt[174]

Watching Your Pit Team in Action

Imagine your management team as the pit crew – your company's growth strategy as the car. Watch how your team works together and engages with the issues of growth performance and potential. This will reveal the level of success that your organization is likely to achieve. There is an exercise in Section 7: The Pit team to help your measure pitstop and pit team effectiveness.

To be a future-focused company... We needed a rhythm to continually identify the right things to review and discuss in order to help us stay focused on the future and avoid being blindsided. And once we found it, this rhythm propelled us forward, past ceiling after ceiling of complexity.

Patrick Thean[175]

SUMMARY

In a VUCA world the pitstop is a powerful model for a more dynamic and agile approach to performance and strategy – an approach that is:

- Agile: Teams start the race with a strategy, but are ready to quickly adapt and to scrap the plan if it is no longer working.

- Market-focused: The team is ready to respond to changing track conditions, or the emerging strategy of a competitor.

- Competitive: It is all about out-maneuvering the competition.

- Goal-oriented: The team shares a common purpose – to make the revenue generating/value creating machine go faster and thereby maximize the chances of winning.

- Highly collaborative: The highly choreographed precision of the pit team of up to 20 people sets the new standard for teamwork and cross-functional collaboration.

- Performance-minded: There is an unrelenting quest for improvement - for the millisecond advantage – both on and off the track. The credo is; you can always go faster.

- Passion-fueled: There is a burning desire to win, with high levels of energy and excitement.

- Action-oriented: Winning the race requires excellent execution, not just a great strategy. There is a heightened sense of urgency – time is precious.

- Innovative: While the team is working to get the most out of this year's car it is already working on a better car for next year. They are continually experimenting and innovating.

All this makes the ability to pitstop an important source of competitive advantage.

SECTION 7

PIT TEAM

The precisely-timed, millimeter-perfect choreography of a modern pitstop is vital to help teams to turn their race strategy into success.

F1.com

INTRODUCTION

It takes a team to race a fast car – that is if it is going to win. The driver cannot just get out of the car and fix it him/herself and one or two people in the pit lane is not enough. It takes a team – a pit team.

Your management team is the pit crew – your organization and its growth strategy is the car. Watch how your team works together and engages with the issues of growth performance and potential. As this section shows this will reveal the level of success that your organization is likely to achieve.

EXTRAORDINARY TEAMWORK

Business and organizational success is increasingly team-based. For example, research shows that a collaborative or team based approach is key to effective strategy and execution[176]. It is also key to learning[177], as well as to innovation and creativity[178]. But what is effective teamwork?

We all have had experience of working with great teams, as well as perhaps some lousy teams too. Yet it can be hard to describe what teamwork is – to make it tangible and put it in words. Thankfully, there is a new way of communicating what great teamwork is, and why it matters. Go to the nearest motor racetrack, or simply type 'pitstop' into YouTube. **To watch the Ferrari™, McLaren™ or Red Bull™ team undertake a pitstop is to witness teamwork at its best**. It is truly awe-inspiring.

A pitstop is a race against the clock. For just a few seconds a driver's success is in the hands of a highly-choreographed pit team of up to 20 people. It looks deceptively easy, but just one person in the wrong place, and 1st place can become 7th place!

Millions of people are watching from their living rooms – a clock at the bottom of the TV screen counts down the milliseconds. One second, wheels off... two seconds, wheels on... three seconds, the car is back in the race. That's it!

pitstop

Noun / **pit•stop** / plural: **pitstops**)

...a stop for fuel and minor repairs during a car race.
...a stop (as during a trip) for fuel, food, or rest
...the new standard for teamwork
...a collaborative & dynamic way of managing performance*

Merriam Webster Dictonary · * Growth Pitstop™ Book

Great pitstops win races; lousy pitstops lose races. What happens when the pit crew comes together determines the outcome of the race. Now research shows that what happens when your management team comes together determines the success of your organization[179].

Your Team   =   Pit Team

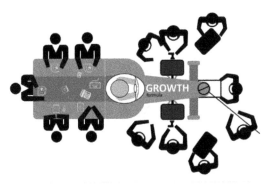

Board Room   =   Pit Lane

Imagine your team working like a pit crew – focused on winning,
working effectively as a team and characterized by urgency and a bias
for action. The pit crew is **the new standard for management team
performance and behavior**.

> *Considering the millions of dollars spent on designing,
> manufacturing and developing a modern Formula One™ car, not
> to mention employing a driver capable of unleashing its
> potential, it's paradoxical that one of the most important parts
> of a Grand Prix comes when the car is stationary.*
> Mark Gallagher[180]

WHY A PITSTOP?

There are two principal reasons to take a pitstop:

- To maximize the chances of winning.
- To minimize the chances of losing.

The first reason to pitstop is to **maximize your chances of winning** -
optimizing the performance of the car, by means of fresh tires and so
on. The second reason is to prevent things happening that could cause
you to lose the race – such as worn tires.   But even if you don't think
you need to take a pitstop to win, you don't have a choice. Presently,
taking a minimum number of pitstops is mandated in F1™. It is just not
deemed safe to push the driver and the car to the limit without a change
of tires and other adjustments being made.

A pitstop is an opportunity to ensure that:

- The nose cone of the car is in good working order (labelled
  Focused Ambition in the Formula for Growth™ - see page 88).

- The wheels are providing good traction (that is Market
  Targeting and Product Fit).

- The steering wheel, which doubles as the driver dashboard and controls, is working reliably (Visibility and Control in the Formula for Growth™).

Can be changed:

Can not be changed:

NO Refuelling

Pitstop What can you change?

Mechanics often say that the adjustments to the car made during a pit stop serve two functions. The first is a technical purpose – that is keeping the car on the track and optimizing its performance. The second is in terms of **the psychology of the driver** – making changes can make the driver feel more in control, or at an advantage. So there is another non-mechanical, but equally important element that can be adjusted in the pit lane: the driver's mindset.

> I want a pit crew… I hate the procedure I currently have to go through when I have car problems.
> Dave Barry[181]

ANATOMY OF A PITSTOP

How quickly the four tires on a F1™ car can be changed is a miracle of the pit lane. If you pull your car into an auto shop to get all four tires changed you could be off the road for an hour or more. In F1™ the car is back on the road in about two seconds – there's no time in the waiting room!

Blink and the pitstop is over! That's what makes a pitstop so impressive. **So much activity by so many people condensed into a mere two seconds**. Pitstops happen so fast that you almost need to see them in slow motion to understand and appreciate the complexity of what happens in the pit lane. So let's go step-by-step through a typical pitstop.

The car has been going 'flat-out' for 10 or 20 laps, reaching speeds of up to 200 mph. The tires have reached pizza oven temperatures and are wearing out fast. Calculations have been made and the timing is right for a pitstop.

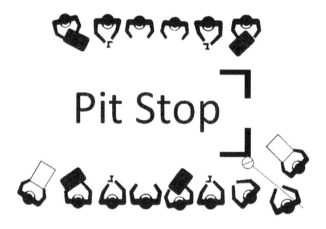

The driver exits the track and reduces speed to 50 mph and below, taking care not to hit any cars or mechanics in the pit lane. He or she proceeds to a designated patch of cement no more than 10 meters squared in front of an open garage. There a pit team of up to 20 people is waiting ready, hearts pounding and fingers itching. Concentration is of the utmost importance.

The driver must stop exactly at the mark, otherwise he/she will hit the person standing ready with a jack to lift the front of the car. The car comes to a sudden stop on the mark and it won't move again until the 'lollipop man' lifts a stop sign he is holding over the car. Meanwhile competitors are continuing to race, as the car is lifted off the ground by a 'jack man' at the front and the rear.

With the car suspended in the air the wheel men begin changing all four tires. That's not easy however – the tires are heavy and hot. It takes three people to execute the procedure at each wheel: one applies the pneumatic wrench, another takes the old tire off, and a third puts the new tire on. **These steps are synchronized** at each wheel – the three-person teams at all four wheels must start and finish together – a situation like that in the diagram below where the different teams are out-of-sequence simply won't work.

⚠ Beware: **out-of-sync pit team**

There has to be perfect alignment or symmetry in the pit lane. The visual representation of the soft parts of the Formula for Growth™ make that clear. As in the diagram overleaf it shows what would happen if there wasn't.

Compare both sides of the pit lane overleaf and highlight any differences that you see.

Then check your team to see if any of the classic signs of misalignment or lack of synergy exist.

Answer: This pit team is the pits! There is a total misalignment between both sides of the pit lane with a total of 10 differences as circled in the diagram. So no matter how well those on the left perform, the car cannot leave until those on the right get their act together. It seems like an extreme example, but there are a lot of organizations where something similar is happening. Take for example the last time your management team came together – were any of the following evident:

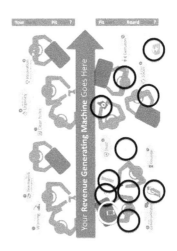

- First-aid box – were there casualties or at least some noses put out of joint?
- Fire-extinguisher – did the meeting get distracted with fire-fighting day to day problems?
- Mobile phone – did anybody take calls or check messages during the meeting?
- Somebody missing – was there somebody missing, arriving late, or leaving early?
- Two people jostling to put on the wheel (top right) – were people roles and responsibilities clear, or did personalities and politics get in the way?
- A person with a hammer instead of a spanner (plus the hand held pump and the oil can) – did everybody have the tools or information that were required to make the meeting a success?

How many of the above indications of misalignment or lack of synergy were evident when your team had its last important meeting, workshop or away-day.

The pit team is a high-bar in terms of teamwork, especially where cross-functional collaboration is required. As those at the coal-face will attest, working in teams can be challenging:

> However brilliant and well-intended your colleagues may be, natural team players they are not. Yet teamwork is imperative to their success, and to yours, too.
> Mark de Rond & Richard Hytner[182]

Executives come together to address fulfil a particular purpose, however their first (and often greatest) challenge is to become an effective team – to become more than the sum of its parts. Yet this gets little attention – the assumption is that bringing people together is enough.

> What may appear like picture-perfect teams are then in reality often quite intricate tapestries of distinct characters united by a common goal but forced into a sanctum where trade-off choices must be made between likability and competence; where powerful but conflicting pressures coexist; where one's success hinges on being able to reconcile camaraderie and rivalry, trust and vigilance, the sacred and the profane; and where they end up getting it wrong as often as right.
> Mark de Rond & Richard Hytner[183]

Pit teams work with choreographed precision – **everybody has their own clear role, yet they are completely interdependent**. A pit team is only as fast as its slowest member. The car cannot exit the pit lane safely until every member of the team has completed their job successfully. It does not matter how great a job the rest of the team does, if one member does not show up, or shows up only to mess-up. It is only when the thumbs-up signal is given from each wheel of the car that the lollipop is lifted and the car can take off.

> *A healthy team is a nimble team. A healthy team can share an insight or idea, then quickly reject or commit to it. This happens when all the disciplines required for a great outcome work collaboratively in real time, not just as a link in a chain of sequential interactions.*
> IBM Design[184]

In addition to the wheel changes other adjustments may be required to the car when it is in the pit lane – for example, replacing the steering wheel or the front nose cone and of course wiping the driver's visor.

How well a pit crew works together is easy to determine. Played out in front of the TV cameras the team's performance is evident to all by reference to a millisecond timer at the bottom of the screen. The speed at which the car exits the pitstop safely into the race is the measure of success. But speed isn't everything. Make a mistake and the result could be a significant penalty, or worse still; injury or even death to one of the pit team, a track official or a spectator.

All that makes the '**precisely-timed millimeter-perfect choreography**' of the pitstop the new standard for teamwork[185].

> Q: *Does your management team work together with the speed, focus and intensity of a pit team?'*

WHY ARE WE MEETING LIKE THIS?

The way we meet reveals a lot about how we collaborate or work as teams. Although executives spend a lot of time in meetings, the research shows that in most organizations managers and their teams don't meet very well. They don't workshop or away-day very well either. For example, executives in our benchmarking group rate their satisfaction with the effectiveness of internal team meetings at just 6 out of 10. However, it is not just team meetings that are struggling with a C grade. What is arguably one of the most important of all meetings - performance reviews - get a broadly similar score. Indeed, it is reflective of the quality of the dialog/interactions between managers and staff which is rated only slightly better at a 68% level of satisfaction. These interactions may be fine for handling the routine day to day activities of the business, but they rarely set 'the world on fire'. So, when it comes to discussions about performance, growth and strategy they are a problem. A lot more is needed. That is a lot more engagement, dialog, innovation and creative problem solving.

> *This basic model works well for the vast majority of meetings: routine check-ins, formal board meetings, planning sessions, and the like. But not when it's time to have an important conversation about critical yet ambiguous issues. That's when you need a more powerful tool.*
> Chris Ertel & Lisa Kay Solomon[186]

Managers often struggle to get their people engaged in a lively debate around performance and potential. These conversations don't happen often enough and when they do typically fall short of the type of discussion that is required. As a result, the meeting organizer is left wondering about the level of engagement, perhaps even commitment, while those attending wonder why they have to waste so much time in meetings that 'go nowhere'. Such gatherings often end up de-motivating rather than inspiring all of those involved.

> *Typically the CEO and his senior leadership team allocate less than half a day each year to review the plans – people, strategy, and operations. Typically too the reviews are not particularly interactive. People sit passively watching PowerPoint presentations. They don't ask questions. They don't debate, and as a result they don't get much useful outcome. People leave with no commitments to the action plans they've helped create. This is a formula for failure.*
> Larry Bossidy *et al*[187]

Most meetings are quite predictable. It's the same agendas, the same people doing most of the talking, the same points being made and the same relatively predictable behaviors and outcomes. Little changes as a result. Crowded meetings across functional silos or teams can be particularly uninspired. There is often more posturing and politics than problem solving, innovation or creativity. The traditional way of meeting may be enough when the stuff that is being talked about is not very important, however when the stakes increase and the conversation must address something as important as the performance, direction or strategy, yet another 'so-so' management meeting or away-day is not going to be enough. A poor quality dialog is going to result in poor strategies and plans, as well as poor execution. It denies the organization the competitive advantage that is the strategic or high-impact conversation.

> ...strategy is a complex, systemic, and open-ended puzzle that cannot be resolved by analysis alone. It's a classic adaptive challenge that calls for a well-designed strategic conversation.
> Chris Ertel & Lisa Kay Solomon[188]

Ineffective Meetings are Expensive

What are ineffective meetings costing your organization, or team each year? That is a question that few managers have stopped to consider. However, do the math – the results (and indeed the waste) will surprise you.

Meetings are expensive, especially unproductive ones. For example, an organization could save the equivalent of almost $300,000 a year in salary-related costs alone if 50 of its executives cut unproductive meeting time by 90 minutes per week. The gross revenue required to pay that amount of salaries would likely be ten to twenty times that figure[189]. The message is a simple one – cut down on the number of unproductive meetings and get the most out of the time that managers are together. That means applying pitstop principles.

The way we meet says a lot about the way we work and even goes a long way to predicting the results we get. But if we change the way we meet we can change the results we get. So, how to run a different more powerful type of meeting - one that is high in impact as well as engagement? Well, the principles are clear. They are to be found in the pit stop.

> *Effective employee communication is a leading indicator of financial performance and a driver of employee engagement. Companies that are highly effective communicators had 47% higher total returns to shareholders over the last five years compared with firms that are the least effective communicators.*
> Towers Watson Inc.[190]

THE PITSTOP CHALLENGE

You don't need a racetrack or overalls to see how well your management team would work as a pit team. Simply bring them together. Ask them to identify a growth accelerator or inhibitor facing the business and to work on addressing it for just one hour. Then stand back and observe.

What unfolds in that room over the next 60 minutes will reveal a lot – not just about what type of pit team you have, but also about the likelihood of winning the race. It will shed a light on team dynamics, such as levels of engagement and commitment, levels of communication and trust, personalities or politics and ultimately standards. What happens in that room is nothing short of an exposé of your organization's growth potential.

To help you understand whether you team reaches the Pit Team standard for performance follow the exercise over the next few pages.

Your Team's Pit Score

Circle the number that best describes your team's performance at its last important meeting and then add up all of the scores.

	Scale	
Poor trust	1 2 3 4 5	High Trust
Poor Communication	1 2 3 4 5	Good Communication
Poor Focus	1 2 3 4 5	Clear Focus
No Urgency	1 2 3 4 5	Maximum Urgency
Low Energy Levels	1 2 3 4 5	High Energy Levels
Poor Teamwork	1 2 3 4 5	Great Teamwork
No Passion Evident	1 2 3 4 5	Passion Highly Evident
Winning doesn't matter	1 2 3 4 5	It's all about winning
Indecisive	1 2 3 4 5	Decisive
Clear Roles	1 2 3 4 5	Confused Roles
Fear	1 2 3 4 5	Courage
Old thinking / Old Solutions	1 2 3 4 5	Creative Problem Solving/Innovation

Calculate your score:

Deduct one point for every time you witnessed any of the following:

- People shouting over each other.

- People not waiting for others to finish their sentences.

- People who were missing, arrived late or left early.

- People checking phones or other devices.

- Each person who tried to dominate the meeting.

- Each person who contributed little, if at all to the meeting.

- Every time somebody pointed the finger of blame at another individual or group.

- Every undiscussable or 'elephant in the room' missing from the discussion.

Add one point for:

- Every respectful challenge.

- Every element of constructive feedback or encouragement.

- Anytime a person said they 'got it wrong', 'it's not working' or 'let's try another approach'.

- Every function, team or business that was represented or at least whose perspective is reflected.

Now check your score:

- Score 45+: Mercedes™ or Red Bull™ want to have your pit team!
- Score 31 to 45: You have a high-performing pit team.
- Score 16 to 30: Pit team in waiting – team development needed.
- Score 0 to 15: Your team is 'the pits' (urban slang for very poor).

Of course there is a simple (and indeed quite accurate) test of your management team interactions: Do they help you, your team and organization to win? A telltale sign is that executives leave meetings and workshops motivated, energized and determined that the team should win. Also that struggling projects, strategies or initiatives gain new momentum, are adjusted or scrapped.

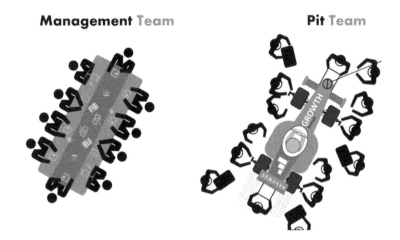

Management Team   **Pit** Team

PIT TEAM REVEALS BUSINESS POTENTIAL

Could the performance of your organization be determined by how well your management team works together? Well, there is mounting research to show that **what happens when your management team gets together reveals the true potential of your organization**. It tells us that the ability of a management team to have an effective dialog about performance – what academics and writers describe as 'hi-impact'[191] or 'strategic'[192] conversations – is a leading indicator of business success.

> *Because groups and teams are the means by which most things get done in organizations, being able to get people to work together more effectively can be the difference between winning and losing in today's competitive business environment.*
> Gordon Curphy & Robert Hogan[193]

The likely success of any growth strategy can be predicted by the quality of the dialog that has shaped its creation. After all, if a team cannot discuss and agree what is or is not working and more importantly what needs to be done, there is little hope for effective strategy, execution or performance. But such a dialog requires a culture of openness, honesty and trust. It requires an environment where people can say what they are thinking – something that is explored in Section 8: The Pit Lane.

The research says that organizations that are able to have such conversations have a competitive advantage over those that cannot.[194] However, it doesn't take research from Harvard or Stanford to show that how managers run their meetings is a reflection of how they run their business. It stands to reason that if a management team cannot dialog effectively for 60 minutes in a room, there is little hope that, outside of the room, they will work cohesively on growing the business. If you want to understand or predict the success of a F1™ team look into the pit lane. If you want to understand and predict the success of your organization look into your management meeting interactions.

> *If an organization's leadership isn't paying close attention to the conversational health of the organization, then it isn't performing one of its most important functions.*
> J.C. Spenser & Bruce A. Strong[195]

Putting the 'T' in Strategy

The number one problem with traditional strategy is the 'Moses Model' where the leader goes off to discover the strategy, writes it in stone and then proclaims it to the masses.

> *'It is no longer possible to figure it out from the top and have everyone following the orders of the 'grand strategist'.*
> Peter Senge & George Roth[196]

But people cannot simply be handed a strategy - there needs to be engagement, ownership and buy-in if the strategy is going to work. A bottom-up approach is required - no longer can strategy be decided by one (or a few people) at the top. It is time to put the 't' (as in 'team') into strategy.

YOUR PIT TEAM

Quarter 4 is approaching fast. You are at lap 35 of a 52-lap race and the pressure is mounting. But if you pull into the pit lane will your team be ready to support you? Will their input help you to win? There is no time for lengthy 'talking shops' and endless meetings. When the team comes together the focus should be on performance and gaining the edge. They should spot what needs to be fixed fast and quickly emerge re-energized, re-focused and primed to win. In short they need to work like a pit crew.   Every time they come together they build momentum, resilience and team cohesion.

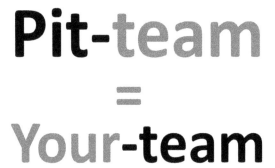

Pit-team
=
Your-team
i.e. those who help you win.
All those who have an important role to play in maximizing the performance and potential of your organization, team, project

A pit team is any team that works together effectively to maximize the chances of winning. But when it comes to growth the ultimate business pit-team is the cross-functional senior management team. Of all the teams in the organization it is the performance of this team that matters most. It holds the promise of the future - the answers to your organization's problems, the strategies for its future growth and the passion to make it happen. So, who is on your pit team for growth and what promise does it bring?

Never doubt that a small group of thoughtful, committed people can change the world. Indeed, it is the only thing that ever has.
Margaret Mead[197]

Where to look for growth?

So what is stopping you? Is it increased competition, more demanding customers, technology, regulation or other factors? Perhaps it is the lack of a clear strategy, poor execution, the motivation or skill of your people, the culture, or leadership of your organization. Maybe it is a combination of these internal and external factors. Regardless, the answer is more and better pitstops. It is there that the innovation, agility and commitment required to accelerate growth is to be found. Test, develop and challenge your management to find the answers by means of effective pitstops.

The world always only changes when a few individuals step forward. It doesn't change from leaders or top-level programs or big ambitious plans. It changes when we, everyday people gathering in small groups, notice what we care about and take those first steps to change the situation.
Margaret J. Wheatley[198]

PITSTOP LEVELS OF PERFORMANCE

Performance in the pit lane comes down to people and in particular how well they work together. That is because despite the sophistication of F1™, pitstops are largely a manual affair. Yes, there are some tools (jacks to lift the car and pneumatic wrenches to change the wheels), but the work is labor-intensive.

A team of up to 20 mechanics and engineers surrounds the car as it comes to a stop. It is called **a pit team, not a pit group** – an important distinction. A pit team is bound together closely in pursuit of a common cause. Ask any member of the pit team what success is and they will give you the same answer. There is a single purpose – a shared vision of success – to win the race by helping the car and the driver to go faster.

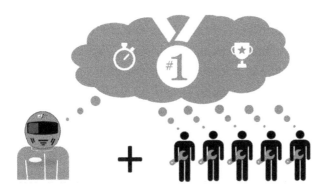

If members do not share a common goal, operate autonomously, or do not share a common fate, then leaders should manage them as a group (not a team).
Gordon Curphy & Robert Hogan[199]

The tag line on F1™ champion Lewis Hamilton's website says it all: "**We win and lose together.**"[200] In F1™ everybody knows where the finish line is and how many laps must be completed to win. However, in organizations there can be different definitions of winning – it depends on whom you ask. In particular goals, priorities and KPIs set at a functional, project and team level often mean that, for one part of the organization to win, another must lose. Internal competition between departments and teams can distract attention from the external competitors in the marketplace.

A pit team is more than a group of individuals. No matter how great the person at the rear wheel wrench is, his efforts alone will not be enough to optimize the car and get it back in the race. Even if he/she is part of a great team at the rear wheel, that still leaves three other wheels to be changed. It is not until the thumbs-up signal is given on each of the wheels that the car can be released from the pit. The same applies to management teams.

A pitstop is the opposite of a one-man show. One person cannot look good, at the cost of others. If the car speeds out of the pit lane while one of its wheels spins off in the direction of the spectators, everybody loses. Either everybody succeeds, or everybody fails. Imagine what would happen if some people turned up with the wrong tools and others showed up with no tools. Worse still if some did not show up at all. That is simply not the pitstop way!

The challenge for organizational leaders is to get their teams performing in a way that is greater than the sum of their individual parts – in other words, to achieve pit crew levels of teamwork.

> *How can a team of committed managers with individual*
> *IQs above 120 have a collective IQ of 63?*
> Peter M. Senge[201]

An organization that depends on heroic solo-runs by individual managers cannot enjoy the same level of sustained success as organizations where there is effective cross-functional teamwork at a management level. Similarly, you cannot accelerate an organization or business unit through a range of sporadic and uncoordinated strategies or initiatives. However, in the absence of effective teamwork at a management level that is exactly what happens and the dominant structure of the organization, characterized by top-down hierarchies and functional silos, doesn't help.

> *Heroic leadership can condition employees to 'look up' passively to the boss instead of 'looking forward' actively to address and conquer the challenges they find within their own sphere of influence, non-adaptive behavior for today's business climate.*

J.C. Spenser & Bruce A. Strong[202]

PIT TEAMS ARE RESPONSE-ABLE

The growth performance and potential of your organization is determined by what happens in the pit lane – specifically how your company responds to the opportunities and challenges of the marketplace is very much a function of your management team and in particular its ability to work together effectively.

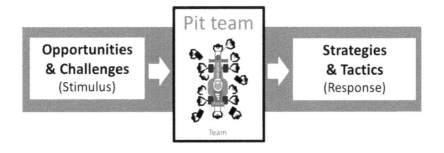

We all like to blame our competitors, marketplace conditions, the shortcomings of suppliers or channel partners and a lack of commitment or skill on the part of particular staff members. However, these are a deflection from where the real responsibility lies. It is the **individual and collective responsibility** of all the members of the pit team (management) to get the car (revenue-generating machine) on the track and to keep it there.

Your management team is responsible for the performance of the organization. Identifying who is responsible is different to looking for who is to blame, however. Saying that the management team is responsible is simply saying the management team has the ability to respond. If your management team does not have the ability to respond then they are not responsible. Here is exactly what that means:

> # Responsibility = respond + ability
>
> (i.e. ability to respond)

The pit team must have control over what happens in the pit lane. There is no point in hiring a pit team and putting them in the pit lane, if they are not going to be able to work on the car. They must be given the tools, the autonomy and the trust to do their job effectively.

> *Between stimulus and response there is a space. In that space is our power to choose our response. In our response lies our growth and our freedom.*
> Victor E. Frankl[203]

In many organizations the ratio of people in the pit lane actively working to make the car go faster versus the numbers standing on the side-lines complaining about the flaws in the strategy, or the skills and commitment of the driver, is completely wrong. Bring the cynics and detractors into the pit lane and get them to share the responsibility for making the car (project, strategy or organization) go faster.

Q: Is there anybody missing from your pit team?

PITSTOP LEVELS OF URGENCY

There is a real sense of urgency in the pit lane. The reason is obvious - when you are standing still in the pit lane, your competitors are racing ahead.

> *They had the soft tyre ready and when the call came they couldn't get the tyres to the car, which probably cost 10 seconds. ...It was gutting to lose a victory like that.*
> Christian Horner[204]

In the 2014 Australian Grand Prix the gap between the winner and the contender was a mere 1.36 seconds. That's why in F1™ the pit teams have to be as fast as their cars.

Every
10 secs
you're in the pitlane...

PIT LANE

...gives your competitors a:
½ Km advantage

Obviously pitstop times vary from team to team – but in a competition where milliseconds matter the driver with the fastest pit team has a real advantage.

2.05 secs
Red Bull **2013 Record**

2.90 secs
Ferrari (2013 Avg.)

3.06 secs
Mercedes (2013 Avg.)

One thing you are unlikely to find in a pitstop is complacency – a pit lane is the ultimate zero-complacency zone. High standards of performance are expected. That is not always the case within organizations where complacency can be a principal cause of strategic failure, especially in large organizations.

> *What is the single biggest error people make when they try to change? After reflection, I decided the answer was that they did not create a high enough sense of urgency.*
> J.P. Kotter[205]

Great teams don't get complacent. Any pit team knows it is only as good as its last pitstop. Once a successful pitstop has been completed the team is already preparing for the next one. However, an organization or team's past success can breed a complacency that dulls its ability to respond to, or perhaps even see, emerging threats in the marketplace. It is a key factor in explaining why new entrants and upstarts are the primary instigators of change in so many industries.

> *Complacency – the odds are overwhelming that there is some around you!*
> J.P. Kotter[206]

Most managers say that there is a high degree of urgency associated with many aspects of their roles. However, it is important to separate strategic urgency from the busyness of day-to-day activity, including meeting deadlines and the occasional fire-fighting, which Harvard's John Kotter calls a false or frenetic urgency.[207] Caught up in the daily or quarterly treadmill of activity, managers can be blinded to looming strategic business opportunities and challenges. As in the pitstop the key is for management teams to focus on what matters most.

Teamwork on Display

The highly choreographed precision of a pit team is the ultimate in teamwork, but how well will your team work together?

Managers build the Formula for Growth™ in a client networking event held by a large consulting client. It gets everybody looking at the complex subject of accelerating sustained and profitable growth in the same way. The result is a powerful dialog about the performance, as well as potential of the organization.

Focusing on organizational health—which we define as the ability of your organization to align, execute, and renew itself

faster than your competitors can—is just as important as
focusing on the traditional drivers of business performance
Scott Keller & Colin Price[208]

PIT TEAM LEVELS OF FOCUS

A pit team is highly-focused. Look into a pit lane and you won't see anybody rubbing his or her chin trying to decide what part of the car to work on. The requirements of getting and keeping the car in the race are clear. The team focuses on what matters and in particular on generating a short-term win.

> *If you could get all the people in an organization rowing in the*
> *same direction, you could dominate any industry, in any market,*
> *against any competition at any time.*
> Patrick Lencioni[209]

A pitstop is about focusing on what matters most. But is that what happens when your management team gets together? Mid-race the car cannot be taken off the track for big repairs. The idea of a pitstop is to speedily optimize the performance of the car and to do so without falling behind in the race. Similarly, management teams cannot afford to divert their attention from the race to deal with the quarter-end or year-end. Fixing things needs to be done fast.

> *Execution is the great unaddressed issue in the business world*
> *today. Its absence is the single biggest obstacle to success and*
> *the cause of most of the disappointments that are mistakenly*
> *attributed to other causes.*
> Larry Bossidy *et al*[210]

In Formula One™ the car is pretty much fixed for the season and big changes are prevented by the F1™ governing body's regulations. So, it is up to the team to **get the most out of the car as it is**, rather than attempt to re-engineer or re-build it. Some things can be fixed in the pit lane, others need to be fixed in the garage (between races) or in the factory (between seasons). Knowing the difference is key – it is important not to 'bite off more than you can chew.' It is all too easy to underestimate the time and other resources required for changes to the car.

> *High-urgency teams guide empowered people to achieve visible, unambiguous short-term wins that silence cynics and critics.*
> J.P. Kotter[211]

The pit lane is a high-pressure environment, with millions watching on their TV sets, and lots of people, bustle and noise creating distraction at the trackside. There is a lot of **noise and interference** within companies too, but unlike pit teams, managers don't have noise reduction headsets.

> *Q: What interference do you observe when your team comes together? What patterns of thinking, behaving and interacting are unhelpful?*

If the pit team is underperforming then the answer is not less time in the pit lane, but more. It is to do more pitstops and to reflect on and learn from each one – getting to know, understand and trust each other more. Just as the secret to great pitstops is a great pit team, the secret to great pit teams is great pitstops. But there is yet another factor – one we will examine in Section 8 – the pit lane environment.

> *When you show up at the track, both your head and your machine should be completely ready to execute the clear plan that you have created. Anything other than that is an unnecessary distraction...*
> Neil Roberts[212]

Before we finish this section take a few moments to reflect on this question:

> Q: *Consider your next team meeting, what will you do to get your team working like a pit crew?*

You may find inspiration in the following quotes from other leading business authors:

> *Building organizations that are deeply adaptable, that are innovative at their core, and that are engaging, exciting places to work—building healthy organizations—requires some deep rethinking about how we put our organizations together.*
> Garry Hammel[213]

> *If good strategy is a function of good conversation, then given the poor state of conversation in many organizations, it's not surprising that the results of strategizing are often disappointing*
> J.-C. Spender & Bruce A. Strong[214]

> *It takes courage to start a conversation. But if we don't start talking to one another, nothing will change. Conversation is the way we discover how to transform our world, together.*
> Margaret J. Wheatley[215]

> *Conversation is the core process by which we humans think and coordinate our actions together. The living process of conversation lies at the heart of collective learning and co-evolution in human affairs. Conversation is our human way of creating and sustaining— or transforming— the realities in which we live.*
> Juanita Brown, David Isaacs, et al.[216]

SUMMARY – THE PITSTOP

The race is on: for every moment your car is off the track, your competitors are passing you by. The growth strategy is the racing car. Your team is the pit crew. People are watching and time is limited. How effectively will they work together to make the car go faster?

The success of a F1™ driver and car depends on the ability of its engineers, designers and pit crew to work effectively together. Failure to execute an effective pitstop is likely to cost the race. With lightning precision the team must envelop the car as it comes to a standstill. In just two seconds the car is lifted, the wheels are changed and the signal is given for the car to accelerate back into the race.

Pitstops are a beauty to watch and pit crews are the ultimate example of teamwork. Their choreographed millimeter–perfect precision sets the new benchmark for high-performing teams. Today's high-performing management teams need the same focus, discipline, speed and teamwork. That makes the pit crew the new standard for team performance and behavioral change.

Imagine if your board meetings, management committees and cross-functional team workshops were conducted with the speed (urgency), focus and teamwork of a pitstop.

The pitstop is about your senior managers coming together and working in a highly-focused and disciplined manner toward a single purpose – improving the performance of your revenue-generating machine (the car). The question is:

Q: What will it take to get your team working like a pit crew and what impact would that have on your organization? Find out by taking the test midway through this section.

Section 8

PIT LANE

Every conversation we hold is an opportunity for discovery, growth, and learning— if not adventure.
John R. Stoker[217]

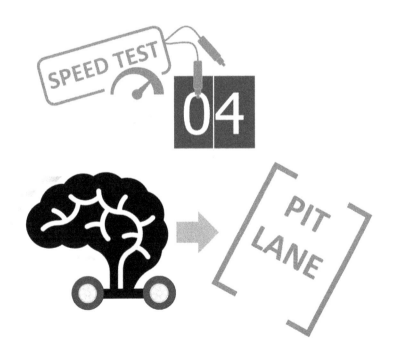

INTRODUCTION

Is the performance of your organization or business unit under pressure from; more demanding customers, increased competition, new technology or new regulations? Well, the answer is in the pit lane. The people who can find it are your pit team. They are also the ones who must execute the changes required to make the solution a success.

The pit lane is the environment in which you and your team work, and most importantly; win together. It is not just the physical space, but also the social, cultural and psychological context. The question is: *Does your team work in an environment that facilitates effective cross functional collaboration, innovation and change?*

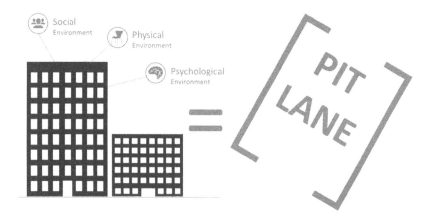

The Pit Lane is all about change. After all there is no point in sending the car (revenue generating/value creating machine) back out the same as it came in – without fresh tires or any of the other important adjustments being made. Yet many managers will point to change as one of the key challenges facing their organizations. In this section we will explore how change takes place in the pit lane as a means of exploring the role of change, learning and innovation in accelerating growth.

CHANGE IN THE PIT LANE

Today we know more about change than ever before. For example, we know that things will naturally stay the way they are (i.e. status quo) unless underlying attitudes and behaviors change. This basic knowledge is key to understanding why so many new projects, initiatives and strategies fail. But it also inspires an approach that can maximize the likelihood of success.

There are invisible markings on the pit lane in every organization. They show the progress of the driver and team in terms of ability to set a strategy and execute it with speed and agility. These markings (shown in the diagram) correspond to the steps required to accelerate and sustain change.

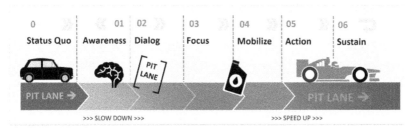

Managers are impatient for change. They want action and they want it now. So they race through the pit lane, or perhaps even bypass it completely. But if you want change – sustainable change, you need to slow down before you can speed up.

A driver must slow the car in order to enable the team to make the necessary changes. The same applies to managers who want growth and the inevitable change it requires. Specifically, to speed up the implementation of your strategies, projects or initiatives you need to slow down and build awareness and dialog. That is the key to successful and sustained change. There are two choices facing the driver - fast in and slow out, or slow in and fast out. The latter is best. It does not mean that the process has to take longer, rather time spent in the early stages should save a lot of time that would otherwise be lost in wrestling with poor execution, and lackluster implementation.

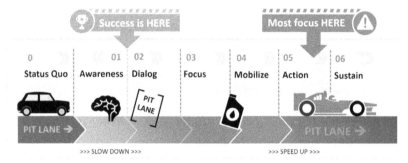

THE PIT LANE STEPS

The pitstop is best seen as a process rather than just an event. It has six steps. You cannot skip a step, otherwise a wheel is likely to come off your strategy, initiative or project as it accelerates onto the track. Let's examine the steps in more detail as the markings on the pit lane.

Step 1:   Awareness.   Managers must slow down to generate awareness of the need for change and the options it presents. This is key to changing attitudes and behaviors, but it requires more than just analysis and information for that to happen. There must be an element of insight and revelation. Typically step 1 happens in parallel with step 2.

Step 2: Dialog.   An open and honest dialog that identifies new solutions and challenges old ways of thinking is the primary ingredient of effective change. It requires engaging with different perspectives, outcomes and alternatives. If done right the process builds commitment and team cohesion. However, an effective team dialog is far from the normal 'broadcast' mode of communication in most organizations. What dialog is and why it matters (more than you think) is explored later in this section.

Step 3: Focus energies, efforts and resources where it can deliver maximum impact. It means focusing on what matters most and often entails trade-offs and compromises. Focus prevents going off in different directions and maximizes the chances of winning.

Step 4: Mobilize. Given the number of false starts that every organization has witnessed, managers need to check that the car (i.e. revenue generating/value creating machine) is ready to be released back into the race. So what do managers need to check before signaling go? Well, anything that could prevent the car pulling away safely and accelerating to top speed. That includes;

- Gathering whatever information is needed and doing the analysis, or running the numbers.
- Addressing any risks, dependencies and key success factors.
- Setting goals and managing expectations.
- Consulting with the relevant stakeholders and getting their buy-in.
- Ensuring that the required resources (in terms of time, budget and manpower) are available.
- Making sure that there is a realistic plan, target and budget in terms of what needs to be done.
- Taking account of competing projects, priorities and initiatives and making sure that the timing is right.

However, the manager can't hold the car in the pit lane until everything is 100% ready. The mobilize stage is about a balance between planning and doing.

Step 5: Action. It is time to hit the accelerator – keeping it there until reaching full speed. That means wholeheartedly and enthusiastically taking action. It requires balancing disciplined and faithful execution of the plan, with an agile/iterative approach and fast learning.

Step 6: Sustain. Starting things is easy, but sustaining them lap after lap can be a challenge, particularly in the face of the inevitable setbacks, distractions and frustrations. It requires reviewing progress, as well as commitment, and re-entering the pit lane to make adjustments. It is a dynamic approach that entails learning and re-learning, managed experimentation and, underpinning it all; a quest for continuous improvement.

The six steps are, in the words of one of our consultants, what makes the difference between a pitstop and a parking space. Put another way if there are problems with implementation and execution, commitment or compliance then it can be tracked back to one or more of the steps of the model. With this in mind check the progress of your change initiative against the model in the diagram overleaf. Have you skipped any steps?

SAFELY LEAVING THE PIT LANE

The use of the Pit Lane in the model of change, learning and engagement is important. That is because the pitstop is about teams taking action to maximize the likelihood of winning – all against the clock. Many managers complain about too much time spent in meetings and workshops. That means the idea of fast pitstops appeals to them. But speed isn't everything.

Have you skipped any steps?

Apply the PitLane Change Model to a project, strategy or initiative to see how effectively the process of change has been managed and developed.

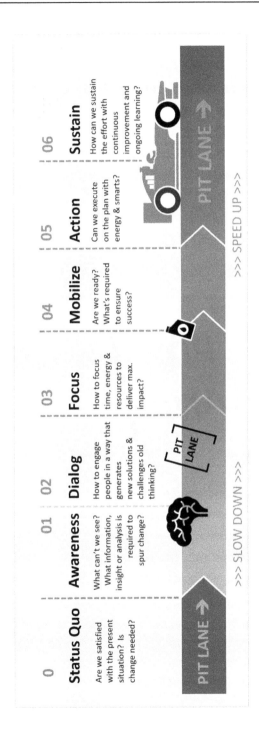

0 Status Quo — Are we satisfied with the present situation? Is change needed?

01 Awareness — What can't we see? What information, insight or analysis is required to spur change?

02 Dialog — How to engage people in a way that generates new solutions & challenges old thinking?

03 Focus — How to focus time, energy & resources to deliver max. impact?

04 Mobilize — Are we ready? What's required to ensure success?

05 Action — Can we execute on the plan with energy & smarts?

06 Sustain — How can we sustain the effort with continuous improvement and ongoing learning?

PIT LANE → >>> SLOW DOWN >>> PIT LANE >>> SPEED UP >>> PIT LANE →

If the driver hits the accelerator before all of the wheels have been fastened the results can be disastrous. There is the costly time penalty, the embarrassment and of course the danger of injury to pit team members, spectators, shareholders, regulators and others. If the nuts haven't been fully tightened on all the wheels, things will get worse before they get better – that is the equivalent of managers making decisions or setting strategy without sufficient analysis, buy-in or consultation.

Take care leaving the [**PIT LANE**]

Problems around implementation, adoption or compliance are the equivalent of losing a wheel after exiting the pitlane. For managers it is an ever present concern. Hence the need to balance the need for fast pitstops with the requirement for a safe car. So, take care leaving the pit lane and don't skip a step.

> *The ability to manage an organization dynamically so that it can both shape its environment and rapidly adapt to it is becoming the most important source of competitive advantage in the twenty-first century.*
> Scott Keller & Colin Price[218]

Modelling Change

Modelling something as complex as change isn't easy. The pit lane model for example is more complex than the diagram might at first suggest. For example, it is not a linear model with discrete neatly ordered steps. Rather there are dotted lines as boundaries - there is an element of awareness, action, dialog and focus in every step and an organization can be in several steps at once. Moreover, the model involves backwards and forwards movement, such as forward from dialog to act and backwards from act to awareness. Most important of all it is an un-ending loop. A pitstop is not just once-off, but rather a process of regular ongoing adjustment based on the constant monitoring of performance. Similarly, for organizations change is a process, not an event. The Pit Stop model for accelerating change has been devised based on:

- Change Models (e.g. Immunity to Change[219] and Hidden Agenda[220])
- Organizational Development (e.g. Patrick Lencioni[221])
- Organizational Learning (e.g. Peter Senge)
- Social Change Principles (e.g. World Café [222])
- Action Learning Principles[223]
- Models of Innovation (e.g. Rowan Gibson[224])
- Coaching Models (such as GROW™[225] and FACT™[226]).

Are you working in a winning environment? That sounds like a strange question, but it is a very important one. Being more specific: Are you working in an atmosphere and culture that is conducive to performing at your best – to winning and succeeding, as an individual and a team?

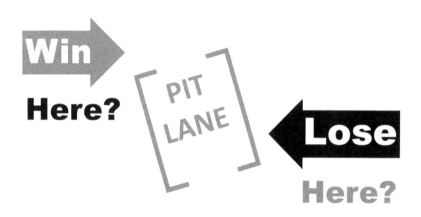

The pit lane environment is very important. But as the diagram below suggests it may be conducive to change, or alternatively limit it. Pressure, tension and miss-trust, for example, can represent dark clouds over any change initiative.

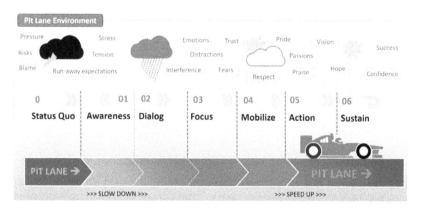

There are many stories in racing of a dramatic change in the fortunes of a once-struggling driver when he or she leaves one team and joins another. Such a turnaround raises the question: if it is the same driver and a very similar car, what makes the difference between a winning streak and a succession of setbacks. Well perhaps there are many factors, but without doubt a change in the organizational and team environment can have a major bearing on the level of success. This applies for managers within organizations, as well as drivers and pit teams within F1™. Yet it is something that can be easily overlooked.

A winning environment is characterized by factors, such as:

- Minimal confusion and politics.
- Constructive or positive internal narrative.
- High morale and productivity.
- Low turnover among good employees.
- People work / pull together.
- Good communication, underpinned by high levels of trust and respect.

Most of us have, at some stage in our career, worked in an organization that was bedeviled with politics, dysfunction, confusion and bureaucracy. These are the characteristics of a losing, rather than a winning environment and we know only too well that they impact on job performance, as well as satisfaction. Such organizations face a performance penalty that can be measured in terms of low productivity, employee turnover, lost innovation, customer attrition and so on. In such organizations it is hard to win.

What happens in the pit lane is one of the most significant points of failure in any business. For example, McKinsey suggests that organizations that ignore health and focus on only performance are 1.5 times more likely to fail in the long run. So, while it is the spectacular high speed crash that gets most attention, the real danger is actually hidden – it is in the pit lane[227].

Organizations and teams that don't have a winning environment face real challenges such as:

☐ People pulling in different directions.
☐ Doubt, anxiety and a lack of confidence.
☐ Confusion and mixed messages.
☐ Poor communication, with low levels of openness & trust.
☐ Fear of change, inertia and lack of innovation.
☐ High levels of politics and turf-wars or boundary disputes.
☐ Protectiveness, defensiveness and blame culture.
☐ Internal competition rather than collaboration.
☐ Confusion about roles, rights and responsibilities.
☐ Poor accountability and reporting.
☐ Negative internal narrative – 'bitching and moaning.'
☐ Group think and stifled innovation.

Has your organization or team got a winning environment? To find out check it against the 12 negative environmental factors listed  above. Tick the ones that are or could be present. If you ticked three or more of the factors then the environment may be hindering your chances of winning.

Are you lucky enough to work within a winning environment? Well, managers rate satisfaction with their working environment at approximately 70% in the Growth Pitstop™ benchmarking data. More specifically here is how satisfied they are with different aspects of their work environment:

- Positive and forward-looking atmosphere (71%).
- High levels of communication, trust and respect (72%).
- Dialog / interactions between managers and staff (68%).
- Fairness of treatment of all staff (75%).
- New ideas welcome, involvement & consultation (79%).

- Support from managers (71%).
- Effective coaching and support (76%).

The question is: *How does your pit lane environment compare with the above benchmarks?*

In times gone by, these factors might have been labeled 'culture' or 'soft stuff' and dismissed as touchy-feely. In more recent times they have been called 'organizational health' and linked to the bottom line.[228] For example McKinsey data suggests that roughly 50 percent of performance variation between companies is accounted for by differences in organizational health[229]. It may therefore be more important than talent, knowledge, or innovation.

> *The single greatest advantage that any organization can achieve is organizational health. Yet it is ignored by most leaders even though it is simple, free and available to almost everybody who wants it.*
> Patrick Lencioni [230]

The implication is that managers need to nurture not just the strategies and skills of their organizations, but also the environment that is required for winning. A driver who has been languishing in one team – spending little or no time on the winner's podium – can become a champion when they move to a new team. When it comes to winning the environment that the driver is in is as important as the car he is driving. It is the leader's responsibility to create and sustain a winning environment, not just for the driver, but the team. They are in effect the Chief Winning Officer and the most important tool they use for this role is good two-way dialog, supported by high levels of trust and respect.

> *No enterprise that lacks robust (organizational) health can thrive for 10, 20, or 50 years and beyond.*
> Scott Keller & Colin Price[231]

There is Wisdom in the Pitlane!

The CEO as the font of all wisdom within the organization is an outmoded and dangerous illusion. Managers have to learn to crowd source their projects and strategies. They must be open to the idea that a diverse group of people can generally find a better solution than any expert.

> If you can assemble a diverse group of people who possess varying degrees of knowledge and insight, you are better off trusting it with major decisions rather than leaving them in the hands of one or two people, no matter how smart the people are.
> James Surowiecki[232]

Moreover, leaders must realize that the process of engaging people in solving their own problems is the most potent means of building capability as well as commitment. It is at the core of the learning organization[233]. Experts will come and go, what matters most is developing internal problem solving capability and expertise. It is a more sustainable and ultimately more successful approach for those who are closest to a problem to be charged with its resolution. After all they are best placed to find the solution that works best.

> ...cloning a product or a service takes no time. But to clone a community takes all the time in the world.
> John Tiefel[234]

WHAT THE PITLANE IS NOT

What makes the difference between winning and losing in the pit lane? Well, to answer this question let's look at what a winning pit lane is not.

Comfort Zone

Silo (Functional)

Talking Shop

Danger Zone

A pit lane is not a comfort zone, a functional silo, a talking shop or a danger zone. Let's explore each of these in turn.

A PITLANE IS <u>NOT</u> A COMFORT ZONE

The pit lane is a challenging place – a high pressure environment where there is no room for complacency, inertia or lethargy. It is a challenging environment. All it takes is for one member of the pit team to slip-up – for example failing to fully tighten one of the wheels – and winning becomes impossible. There is no sitting on the team's laurels when the pitstop is over, the countdown to the next pitstop is already underway. A team is only as good as its last pitstop.

Optimal conflict: the persistent experience of some frustration, dilemma, life puzzle, quandary, or personal problem that is perfectly designed to cause us to feel the limits of our current way of knowing.
Robert Kegan & Lisa Laskow Lahey[235]

The next stage of your organization's growth lies just beyond its comfort zone – beyond what is easy, familiar and certain. It requires the courage to:

- Provoke debate
- Cause reflection
- Embrace change
- Question assumptions
- Challenge old ways of thinking
- Discuss the 'undiscussables'
- Entertain multiple scenarios/outcomes
- Tolerate some anxiety
- Seek outside views
- Generate respectful challenge
- Listening to discordant voices
- Stir things up – break with convention
- Experiment and take risks
- Discuss performance openly and honestly
- Entertain that there may be a better way and that we can or should do better.

There is no single right answer to the business opportunities and challenges facing organizations in an increasingly complex and fast changing world. Today's strategies require engaging multiple perspectives and seeking out contrary opinions. They also require challenging the status quo. Teams must avoid group think, cozy consensus and the lure of the status quo.   They must seek disconfirming evidence, challenge assumptions and listen to the lone voice in the wilderness (even when it is annoying).

> *Part of the new playbook for strategy is to... seek out disconfirming evidence. The idea is to create an environment in which people can share evidence that things may be changing and thereby spark action. This can be easier when it is obvious that the organization is in trouble—it's much harder when things seem to be going well, at least on the surface.*
> Rita Gunther[236]

Danger in the Pit Lane!

The pit lane can be a dangerous place. There are fast moving cars, intense pressure, heavy lifting and of course lots of noise. Yet, F1™ is leading the way in terms of Health and Safety[237]. If only management team pitstops could be conducted in a similarly safe environment – one that would ensure open communication, high levels of trust and collaboration. Only in such an environment can people:

- Say what they are really thinking
- Offer an alternative perspective
- Respectfully challenge conventional wisdom and each other
- Suggest the 'hair-brained' idea that could cause a revolution
- Break free of a cozy consensus or group think
- Say they were wrong, without fear of criticism.

Trailblazers aren't driven by keeping score but are motivated instead by the belief that great work is done together, that efficiency is gained by trust and that safety opens the floodgates of the mind. They have everything to teach us – and sharing is what they do best.
Margaret Heffernan[238]

Getting the balance right between a challenging and a cozy environment is key:

> *The best conditions for thinking, if you really stop and notice, are not tense. They are gentle. They are quiet. They are unrushed. They are stimulating but not competitive. They are encouraging. They are paradoxically both rigorous and nimble. Attention, the act of listening with palatable respect and fascination, is the key to a Thinking Environment.*
> Nancy Kline[239]

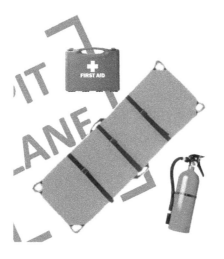

An Effective Open Dialog requires a Hi-Trust Environment

> *Too much challenge and not enough safety = stress. Too little challenge and too much safety = boredom. Lack of challenge is as bad (if not worse) than too much.*
> W. Timothy Gallwey[240]

A PITLANE IS <u>NOT</u> A TALKING SHOP

'Less talk and more action' is a refrain often heard within organizations. Typically, however the problem isn't too much talking, but the absence of an effective dialog. That is the type of engaging, challenging and insightful dialog that goes beyond the typical transitionary exchanges within most organizations.

You will remember that 'Dialog' is the second step in the Pit Lane change model. It is arguable the most important, as well as the most commonly neglected. Increasingly research suggests that many of the challenges facing a modern business can be traced back to the quality of its internal dialog. So, while talk maybe cheap, effective dialog is priceless. Organizational Health is a leading indicator of business performance. It is manifest in the pit lane and how well your cross functional management team works together as a pit team. There the quality of the dialog / conversation can clearly be seen.

Quality of Dialog Drives Business Performance

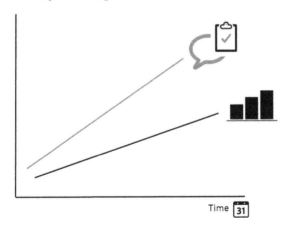

Q: What would you do differently if you believed that the ability to have an open and honest dialog drove business performance?

In their quest to accelerate growth managers are busy driving the car (i.e. the strategies, processes and structures of growth). However increasingly the research shows that it is the dialog that really drives performance.

> *...it could be said that all great failures in practical and professional life stem from parallel failures in this single domain of conversation. The problems that even the most practical organizations have—in improving their performance and obtaining the results they desire—can be traced directly to their inability to think and talk together, particularly at critical moments.*
> William Isaacs[241]

Managers will say that they are constantly communicating with colleagues but that is not the same as having an effective dialog. It is important to distinguish between a discussion and a dialog. Moreover, to understand that dialog isn't just about talking (or talking and listening) – it is about thinking and re-thinking together. Effective dialog results in new insights and new ideas. It spurs, rather than stalls action. It is the essential primer for change and innovation.

> *...the conversation couples together the people with power-to-perceive, those with power-to-think and those with power-to-act. All three are necessary in a good strategic conversation. All three roles have an essential part to play.*
> Kees van der Heijden[242]

For hard-nosed managers dialog can at first seem soft. Yet it is not just about having nice conversations, 'feel-good sessions' or 'love-ins' as managers might cynically describe them. It is about having the tough and unpleasant conversations too – those are arguably the most important conversations of all. Indeed, it is how teams discuss the set-backs, disappointments and frustrations that is most revealing. It is when the 'stakes are high' that an effective dialog matters most. So the question is: *How does your team engage with the topics that are most challenging and contentious?*

Pit teams at the race track work with wrenches and jacks, while the key tool used by management pit teams is effective dialog. That is a powerful and versatile tool, but while it is capable of solving almost any problem it is little known or used. Moreover, it requires a skilled operator.

Dialog Anxiety

Managers often express pre-pitstop anxiety in the form of concerns about the nature of the dialog:

- Will the conversation become negative?

- Will some people dominate the conversation?

- Will people complain rather than take responsibility for what they themselves can do?

These anxieties suggest that managers are wrestling with the role of dialog, or how it should be facilitated, and more fundamentally a reluctance to trust people with something as dangerous as words! As a consequence, they often side step important conversations as a result. However, the real problems begin when people don't say what they are thinking - either because they don't care enough, or because they are afraid of the consequences of saying the wrong thing. The cost of silence should not be underestimated[243].

> *What Is the Cost of Silence? No results is the cost of silence! You may get more of the same, or things may get worse. The advantages for speaking up far outweigh keeping your mouth shut and your head in the sand.*
> John R. Stoker[244]

What is the difference between a discussion and a dialog? Take the last important issue addressed in your organization – did it involve an effective dialog or simply a discussion. Use the table below to find out.

EXERCISE

	Discussion	Dialog
Why?	Arriving at a decision or agreed action(s) within a set time frame and set agenda.	Seeks new insights, breakthroughs, solutions, creative problem solving and high levels of engagement.
When?	Day to day interactions.	When the people and/or the issue really matter. When it is complex, challenging or strategic. It is often not just about one conversation. Check periodically to see that the dialog is working for everybody.
What?	Agenda driven with specific outcome(s) in mind.	An effective dialog is free-flowing. It starts with an important topic / set of questions to be explored. There is a high level of openness - people can speak freely.
How?	Talking (backwards and forwards), discussing and presenting.	People are not just talking – they are thinking (and re-thinking) together. Really listening to what each other is saying and reflecting on what one is saying oneself. Requires high levels of self-awareness and self-control.
Where?	Environment matters little. Formal meeting environment around a table.	A conducive environment/ atmosphere; clean, bright, comfortable seating and so on.
Who?	Seniority or rank determines the conversation.	Giving everybody a chance to talk - treating all ideas openly. Welcome diverse perspective & discordant views.
Skill?	Every day skills.	Coaching & facilitation, listening, self-awareness, re-framing, etc.

What is required to enable a new deeper conversation regarding success? Well one key measure of the effectiveness of the dialog in the pit lane is respectful challenge. People have to be able to express disagreement, doubt or uncertainty. That requires creating a safe place for "Not Knowing"[245], admitting 'we got it wrong' or entering the Zone of Uncomfortable Debate.[246] All this makes courage an important ingredient of an effective dialog.

Effective dialog is about learning at the most important level of all; the team. So the pit lane dialog is the means of organizational learning, as well as the development of individual and team confidence, capability and resilience. So if a team is broken in any way the answer is not for it to spend less, but rather more time working together. That means more pitstops. Just as in any other arena, practice in the pit lane makes perfect.

> *Team learning is vital because teams, not individuals, are the fundamental learning unit in modern organizations. This is where the rubber meets the road; unless teams can learn, the organization cannot learn.*
> Peter M. Senge[247]

Q: How effective is the dialog about performance and potential in your organization (on a scale of 1-10, where 1 = 'very poor' and 10='very good')? What would you like the score to be?

Look Back into the Pit Lane

Many managers have great conversations with mentors, coaches and consultants, but not with their teams. They get their ideas in conversation with outsiders, rather than with their teams - arguably the most important conversations of all. They invest in their own personal learning - doing courses and reading books for example. But they don't learn, develop and grow with their teams - arguably the most powerful learning of all. Not only do both of these scenarios represent a lost opportunity for the organization, they can result in increased distance and even frustration between the manager and the rest of the team as the manager travels the journey of learning alone. The message is look in your pit lane for ideas, challenges and inspiration. If you don't think you will find it there then invest in the pit team you have, or start to build a new one.

A PIT LANE IS <u>NOT</u> A SILO

A pit lane cannot be a silo. Each person has their own job to do, but they are also totally interdependent. Most importantly everybody shares **a common goal and a shared definition of winning**. That makes the pit team a model for cross-functional teamwork within organizations where a top-down hierarchal structure combined with functional silos makes effective cooperation across business departments, units and teams a challenge. In these environments managers with their own priorities, projects and KPIs can easily lose sight of the bigger prize. The result is internal competition rather than cohesion.

> *Top-down hierarchies... where positions of authority become scarce resources. ...Members withhold or hoard information by focusing competition energy internally rather than externally, creating silos of information and causing the negative stress...* Janna Raye Petaluma[248]

Silos restrict growth. It takes a team to build and maintain a great car (revenue generating/value creating machine). The C-suite pit lane is a place for cross-functional collaboration. Managers need to come out of their silos if they are to work effectively on accelerating growth. This is all the more important where management teams are homogenous and as a result can suffer from blinkered thinking, or even group think. The variety of insights and experience presented by a diverse and cross-functional team is important to innovation and growth. Indeed any cross-functional team can benefit from adopting a pitstop mindset – for example research in hospitals suggests it can reduce certain errors by 30%.[249] The message for managers is clear: **success is cross-functional, so too is growth**.

Q: If you believed that cross-functional collaboration was essential to winning how would you engage with your colleagues?

> *Strategizing depends on creating a rich and complex web of conversations that cuts across previously isolated knowledge sets and creates new and unexpected combinations of insight.*
> Gary Hamel[250]

In reality collaboration presents challenges and it often runs counter to both organizational culture as well as form. Moreover, research warns that power dynamics matter and that the higher you move up an organization the more difficult collaboration can become[251]. Creating the conditions for effective collaboration requires deliberate steps, including directly addressing the costs, benefits and risks of collaborating for all those involved.

> *Cooperation between individuals with distinct responsibilities, resources, and constraints always involves what we call adjustment costs.*
> Yves Morieux and Peter Tollman[252]

In many organisations there is a powerful source of new ideas and diversity that remains untapped. That is the diversity that exists between different functions – such as marketing and operations for example, or finance and I.T. People within these different functions think and talk differently, there are often even different personality types involved. Harnessing this source of diversity has the potential to accelerate growth and innovation.

Multidisciplinary teams aren't just faster—they're smarter…Put people new to the problem alongside those with deep working knowledge. If you're in doubt about who to include, err on the side of including new and different perspectives.
IBM Design[253]

Diversity in the Pit Lane

Diversity has been on the corporate social agenda for some time, yet the C Suite stubbornly remains homogenous. Too many boardrooms are populated by grey-haired and balding Caucasian males in dark suits. While we espouse diversity, without even being aware of it, we seek out those who look like us, talk like us and think like us. This reflects our innate tribal bias as human beings, or subconscious attraction to the familiar - to those that are like us. But that makes us subject to group think and cosy consensus and thus vulnerable to change.

Human beings want to feel good about themselves and to feel safe, and being surrounded by familiarity and similarity satisfies those needs very efficiently. The problem with this is that everything outside that warm, safe circle is our blind spot.
Margaret Heffernan[254]

'They just could not see it coming' – that is the message presented by those who write about big corporate failures. They surrounded themselves with (and benchmarked against) people who saw the world the way they did, silenced the sceptics and could (or would) not see the writing on the wall. When they did it was too late. Hence the importance of diversity in the C-Suite pit lane. Engaging multiple perspectives is vital to business agility and innovation – to sustained and profitable growth. But how well does your team leverage diversity?

…the better the knowledge flows and the more relevant perspectives brought to bear, the more opportunity there is for innovation.
J.-C. Spender & Bruce A. Strong[255]

A PLACE FOR PASSION

There is one last thing that we always look for in the pit lane. That is passion. If the passion is missing from the pit lane then it is going to be missing from the factory floor, the next team meeting, the next big customer meeting and just about everywhere else.

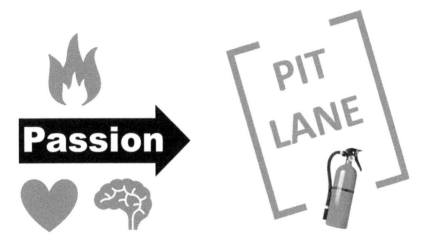

The passion may be evident in enthusiasm and energy, or alternatively in anger, frustration, or fear. The latter in particular can scare managers. However, the real problem is when the passion is absent. A pit lane is no place for the half-hearted.

> In a high-stakes situation, the prevailing language shifts to an emotional, symbolic, mythic form: the language of heroes and villains, of confrontation and suffering, malevolence and primal desires.
>
> Peter M. Senge[256]

The level of passion exhibited by management and leadership teams sets the cue for the level of passion exhibited throughout the organization. Passion is contagious. That puts displaying their own passion and igniting the passion of others as an important requirement of pit lane success.

> *Those who argue that business decisions made by managers are, or indeed should be 100% logical and analytical are overlooking one key fact. Business decisions cannot be isolated from the social and cultural environment within which they take place.*
> Dan Ariely[257]

War for Talent or Battle for Engagement?

There is much talk of the war for talent[258]. That is the scramble by organizations to hire the 'A' players in their industry, often by tempting them away from a competitor. In doing so many organizations may be fighting the wrong battle – especially if you believe that passion and engagement, rather than talent, are the real mark of victory. The question is can you win on talent acquisition and then lose on passion and engagement? There is evidence that this happening in many organizations.

THE PHYSICAL PLACE

A Pit Lane in F1™ is where pit stops take place - where essential mid-race modifications and adjustments are undertaken in order to maximize the chances of winning. In business a pitstop is where the managers come together as a team to review the performance of key growth related strategies, projects and priorities and to optimize their success. The corporate Pit Lane is the physical space where project reviews, management meetings, strategy workshops and away-days take place.   That is the conference rooms, executive suits and boardrooms where the important executive dialog takes place.

The environment in which learning, engagement and discussion take place is important. It should be a comfortable space, a creative space – a winning space. The environment clearly has an influence on how the conversation and the ideas will flow. Yet organizations often book a meeting room – either onsite or offsite - with little consideration. Corporate meeting spaces are often uninspiring and even uncomfortable. For example, here is a note displayed prominently in the meeting suite of a major financial Institution. It might as well say no learning, no creativity and most important of all NO FUN!

 **DON'T**

 DO:

- ☒ Don't put posters and blue tack on the walls
- ☒ Don't bring cups of coffee in to the room
- ☒ No food or refreshments in the room
- ☒ Don't move/remove any furniture
- ☒ Don't adjust the A/C it is automatically set

- ☑ Rooms must be booked at least 24 hours in advance
- ☑ Keep noise levels to a minimum
- ☑ Tidy up when you finish
- ☑ Turn off lights when you leave

Look into a meeting space and you get a pretty good idea of the type of conversations that are taking place there – the typical business discussion or a richer and more transformative dialog. Where you meet says a lot about the process of dialog in your organization, including how important and how effective it is. So take a look at the physical environment in which your important meetings and workshops take place.   What does it say about the quality of the dialog in your organization? Is it conducive to high levels of engagement, creativity and most important of all - an effective dialog?

> *Create a particular environment, and people will think for*
> *themselves. It is that simple.*
> Nancy Kline[259]

Improving the physical space in which people meet can give a boost to the level of dialog and engagement. It should be an environment that is reflective of the importance of the work being done and the pride that people have in doing it. The basics are that it should be clean and tidy with natural light and good ventilation. It should be spacious and comfortable. Plus, there should be drinks and snacks, not just the sugary ones either. Try taking out the tables! Putting in more comfortable seats. Adding some nice décor, some plants and letting some natural light in.

> *Most individuals can't seem to recognize the undercurrents*
> *beneath the surface of their conversations, undercurrents that*
> *can bring people together or tear them apart.*
> William Isaacs[260]

ARE YOU UP TO THE CHALLENGE?

The ability of managers within an organization to have an effective dialog about performance (as well as potential) is an important source of competitive advantage. It also drives business results. But it is not easy however. If it was every organization would be doing it and dialog would no longer serve to separate the average from the great.

The conversational health of many organizations is poor. It is not something that managers are taught about. Moreover, for most, engaging in effective dialog would require significant attitudinal and behavioral adjustment.

One of the components of a Thinking Environment is equality. Another is listening with respect and without interruption. Another is removing limiting assumptions. Another is appreciation. This means that everyone at certain points, including at the beginning, has a turn to speak without interruption and with respectful attention from everyone else.
Nancy Kline[261]

Don't forget Eddie Jordan!

'Don't forget Eddie Jordan!' is a favorite saying among pitstop facilitators and consultants, referring to the Irish-born TV commentator and former F1™ team owner. The message is a simple one – make sure that the person who ultimately owns the car is involved. Great pitstops depend on it. There is no point in a team of enthusiastic managers or team members identifying lots of ways to improve the strategy and its execution, only to find that the person in charge doesn't get it. Involving the ultimate decision-maker is key to success.

...conversation trumps structure. Rearranging the hierarchy won't save a company in poor conversational health. Nonetheless, flatter organizations are typically less rigidly formal and less siloed, which helps to promote strategic conversations.
J.-C. Spender & Bruce A. Strong[262]

SUMMARY

Winning doesn't just take place out in the marketplace, or on the launch of a great strategy. It begins back in the executive suite when managers and their teams meet to plan and review key projects, initiatives and strategies. That is in the pit lane.

It is no great mystery why so many great initiatives, projects and strategies fail to be implemented successfully. Indeed, the requirements of successful change, learning and innovation can be mapped out on the floor of the pit lane.

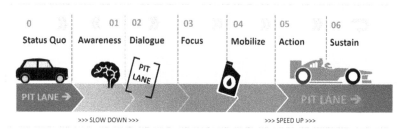

Problems around implementation, adoption or compliance are the equivalent of the losing a wheel after exiting the pit lane. For managers it is an ever present concern.

Managers are impatient for change. They want action and they want it now. So they race through the pit lane, or perhaps even bypass it completely. But if you want to speed up the implementation of your strategies, projects or initiatives you need to slow down and build awareness and dialog (steps 1 and 2). That is the key to successful and sustained change.

Improving the quality of conversations (awareness and dialog) among teams is a powerful way of boosting business performance. Perhaps the most effective means. It requires moving from ineffective discussion to an effective dialog. That is a real challenge for all involved.

Pay attention also to the pit lane environment – make it a physical and psychological space for winning. That includes getting the right balance between safety and challenge in the pit lane.

MORE PIT LANE INSPIRATION

The topics of change, organizational dialog and learning are vast. With that in mind here are some inspirational and challenging quotes that might guide you to other writers on the subject:

> *You cannot plan in silos. We get things done faster and more efficiently when our priorities are complementary.*
> Patrick Thean[263]

> *Indeed, almost everywhere I looked in the financial crisis it seemed that tunnel vision and tribalism had contributed to the disaster. People were trapped inside their little specialist departments, social groups, teams, or pockets of knowledge. ...how foolishly people can behave when they are mastered by silos.*
> Gillian Tett[264]

> *One of the most important shifts required in this new way of viewing conversation is to re-evaluate our traditional view that talk and action are separate activities.*
> Juanita Brown, David Isaacs, et al.[265]

> *As large companies had become more structured around divisions and business units and consequently developed into silos, so the use of cross-disciplinary multifunctional teams became a means of bridging the gaps...*
> Tim Jones, Dave McCormick & Caroline Dewing[266]

> *Growth is not just a concern of sales and marketing, but of product, engineering and support too. It is this organization-*

wide commitment to growth that ultimately sets these companies apart.
Sean Ellis & Morgan Brown[267]

In dialog, there is the free and creative exploration of complex and subtle issues, a deep "listening" to one another and suspending of one's own views. By contrast, in discussion different views are presented and defended and there is a search for the best view to support decisions...'
Peter M. Senge[268]

At IBM, we have a saying: "Empathy: first with each other, then with our users."
IBM Design[269]

The intention of dialog is to reach new understanding and, in doing so, to form a totally new basis from which to think and act. In dialog, one not only solves problems, one dissolves them. We do not merely try to reach agreement, we try to create a context from which many new agreements might come. And we seek to uncover a base of shared meaning that can greatly help coordinate and align our actions with our values.
William Isaacs[270]

...we've found patterns of communication to be the most important predictor of a team's success. Not only that, but they are as significant as all the other factors - individual intelligence, personality, skill, and the substance of discussions — combined.
Alex "Sandy" Pentland[271]

Can You Recognize Undiscussables? Undiscussables are easy to recognize, whether they are your own or someone else's. When you see negative emotion, hear blame stories, or notice that everyone is talking about a problem except the person who needs the feedback, you know that undiscussables are in control.
John R. Stoker[272]

SECTION 9

CONCLUSION & ACTIONS

Motor racing is a sport that brings people to the limit: men and machine...
Ayrton Senna[273]

INTRODUCTION

As the book is now coming to an end it is time to accelerate – just like you would out of a pitstop. It is time to take the ideas and insights onto the track and put them to work for your success.

> Section One of this book was written to serve the dual purpose of acting as an Executive Summary as well as an Introduction. So, if you would like a summary of the book you might like to go there. This section is a little more pointed – it is aimed at eliciting how you will put the lessons on speed and winning in F1™ to work in accelerating the growth of your organization, business unit or team.

A great driver requires a great machine, which in turn requires great pitstops and an effective pit team. The environment in which these come together – the pit lane - is important too. These are the 4 Speed Tests and they are as relevant to the boardroom as the race track. But how will you leverage these secrets to accelerate the growth of your organization, business unit or team? Let's find out.

SPEED TEST 1: **MACHINE**

A driver can only go as far and as fast as his, or her vehicle will take them. For a CEO the organization's business units, divisions and teams are the vehicles of growth – they are the revenue generating / value creating machines. But how to make them go / grow faster?

Q: Will you work to improve the power and performance of your organization's Revenue Generating (or Value Creating) Machine?

Using the table below rate the performance of your organization or business unit's revenue generating/value creating machine in the left

column. Then in the right column set a goal for what you want to improve that rating to over the next 12 months?

Today's Score (1=very poor, 10= excellent)	Speed Test 1: Your Revenue Generating / Value Creating Machine	Your Goal (1=very poor, 10=excellent)
10		10
9		9
8		8
7		7
6		6
5		5
4		4
3		3
2		2
1		1
What benefits will this improvement deliver?		
Quantify the potential impact (%) on growth:		

To complete the table list some of the benefits that you expect from achieving this goal. Finally quantify the potential impact (%) and set about planning the actions you can take. In terms of setting your rating or goal for this area you might like to refer back to Section 5: The Growth Machine (Speed Test 1).

If you have chosen to work on Speed Test 1 (the Race Machine), enter into a dialog with your Pit Team about what is in the table; the rating today, the goal for the future, as well as the potential benefits and impact. Then discuss solutions, ideas and actions and in particular how to improve the performance of your revenue generating/value creating machine:

- Will your team work on precision (and profitability) at the **front of the machine**? That is the nose cone representing 'Focused Ambition' (i.e. Priorities, Resources & Commitment) and the direction setting variables of strategy as the front wheels of the car (i.e. 'Product Traction' and 'Market Targeting').

- Will your team work on the back of the car and its power to acquire, as well as to retain and grow customers? In particular revving up the **sales and marketing engine** and at the same time improving its effectiveness and efficiency.

- Will your team work on your systems, structures, processes and reporting in order to ensure improved **visibility, predictability and control** as you accelerate growth?

  A racing car is an animal with a thousand adjustments.
  Mario Andretti[274]

SPEED TEST 2: **PITSTOP**

Winning a motor race depends on the ability to quickly pull the car into the pit lane and to perform essential improvements without falling behind. The same applies to your Revenue Generating / Value Creating Machine - its key strategies, projects and plans require effective pitstops on a regular basis. The question is:

Q: Will you and your team take more and better pitstops?

Using the table below rate your organization or business unit in terms of its ability to pitstop **EXERCISE**
effectively in the left column. Then in the right column set a goal for what you want to improve that rating to over the next 12 months?

Today's Score (1=very poor, 10=excellent)	Speed Test 2: Your Pitstops (i.e. how key growth strategies, projects and initiatives are reviewed and adjusted)	Your Goal (1=very poor, 10=excellent)
10 9 8 7 6 5 4 3 2 1		10 9 8 7 6 5 4 3 2 1
What benefits will this improvement deliver?		
Quantify the potential impact (%) on growth:		

To complete the table list some of the benefits that you expect from achieving this goal. Finally quantify the potential impact.

The pitstop is the means by which driver and machine can address performance issues and adapt to changing track conditions, the moves of a competitor and so on. In terms of your rating or goal for this area you might like to refer back to Section 6: the Pitstop.

If you have chosen to work on Speed Test 2, enter into a dialog with your Pit Team about what is in the table - the rating today, the goal for the future, as well as the potential benefits and impact. Then discuss solutions, ideas and actions and in particular explore:

Q: How to pitstop key growth strategies, projects and initiatives in a way that will help to win more/better?

> *Considering the millions of dollars spent on designing, manufacturing and developing a modern Formula One™ car, not to mention employing a driver capable of unleashing its potential, it's paradoxical that one of the most important parts of a Grand Prix comes when the car is stationary.*
> Mark Gallagher[275]

SPEED TEST 3: **PIT TEAM**

The machinery of business is only as powerful as the pit team that maintains and supports it. Similarly, the growth performance and potential of your organization depends on your senior managers working effectively as a pit team. The question is:

Q: Will you invest in, support and develop your pit team?

Using the table below rate the performance of your organization or business unit's senior management team as a pit crew in the left column. Then in the right column set a goal for what you want to improve that rating to over the next 12 months?

Today's Score (1=very poor, 10=excellent)	Speed Test 3: Your Pit Team (i.e. cross functional senior management team)	Your Goal (1=very poor, 10=excellent)
10		10
9		9
8		8
7		7
6		6
5		5
4		4
3		3
2		2
1		1
What benefits will this improvement deliver?		
Quantify the potential impact (%) on growth:		

To complete the table list some of the benefits that you expect from achieving this goal. Finally quantify the potential impact.

The highly choreographed precision of the pit team sets the new standard for teamwork and cross-functional collaboration. It exemplifies; leadership, urgency, discipline, trust and a passion for winning. While each person on the pit team has their own role and responsibilities, they are interdependent rather than independent and all share the same goal; making the car / organization go faster. In terms of your rating or goal for this area you might like to refer back to Section 7: The Pit Team (Speed Test 3).

> *The driver is one part of a team, and in order to sustain success in this highly competitive situation all aspects of the team have to integrate effectively.*
> Mark Jenkins, Ken Pasternak & Richard West [276]

If you have chosen Speed Test 3, enter into a dialog with your Pit Team about what is in the table; the rating today, the goal for the future, as well as; the potential benefits and impact. Then discuss the following question:

Q: *How to support and develop the pit team so as to enable the business to go / grow faster?*

> *I'm really grateful to have had the opportunity to be out front... It's a very special feeling to have such an amazing car, and team...*
> Lewis Hamilton [277]

SPEED TEST 4: **PIT LANE**

The pit lane is where it all comes together;
the driver, race machine, pitstop and pit team. The corporate pit lane
is the environment in which a team works, and most importantly; wins
together. It is not just the physical space, but also the social, cultural
and psychological context.

Q: Will you create an environment conducive to winning?

*Using the table overleaf rate your
organization or business unit's pit lane as it is
today in the left column. Then in the right*

*column set a goal for what you want to improve that rating to over the
next 12 months? Next list some of the benefits that you expect from
achieving this goal. Finally quantify the potential impact.*

Today's Score (1=very poor, 10=excellent)	Speed Test 4: Your Pit Lane (the cultural, political & physical environment for cross functional collaboration, learning & innovation in your organization)	Your Goal (1=very poor, 10=excellent)
10		10
9		9
8		8
7		7
6		6
5		5
4		4
3		3
2		2
1		1
What benefits will this improvement deliver?		
Quantify the potential impact (%) on growth:		

The race pit lane is a high pressure environment with lots of noise, heat and of course; fast moving vehicles. The same applies in organizations where personalities, politics and competing priorities distract from an open and honest dialog regarding performance and potential. In terms of your answer to the above question you might like to refer back to Section 8: The Pit Lane (Speed Test 4).

If you have chosen to work on Speed Test 4, enter into a dialog with your Pit Team about what is in the table; the rating today, the goal for the future, as well as; the potential benefits and impact. Then discuss solutions, ideas and actions and in particular: *How to develop a winning environment?*

> *Winning teams have the least amount of distractions. They have a really tight group of people working towards the same common goal.*
> Larry Dixon[278]

DEVELOP THE CHAMPION DRIVER!

Let's not forget the 'not-so-secret' Speed Test – you need a great driver – a Michael Schumacher or Lewis Hamilton. That of course is you!

Q: Will you work to further develop yourself as a Michael Schumacher or Lewis Hamilton within your organization?

Rate yourself as a driver in your organization today on the left column of the table overleaf. Then in the right column set a goal for what
you want to improve that rating to over the next 12 months? Next list some of the benefits that you expect from achieving this goal. Finally quantify the potential impact.

Today's Score	The 'not-so-secret' Speed Test The Champion Driver	Your Goal
10		10
9		9
8		8
7		7
6		6
5	= YOU	5
4		4
3		3
2		2
1		1
What benefits will this improvement deliver?		
Quantify the potential impact (%) on growth:		

Make a list of the actions you will take to improve your performance as a Champion Driver and where you will go for information, inspiration or help.

> *I know what it takes to be fast and I feel like every year I learn valuable lessons about how to be better the next time.*
> Danica Patrick[279]

BACK TO THE ULTIMATE QUESTION

You will remember that this book began by asking what was called 'the ultimate question': *What percentage of your company's full growth potential is presently being exploited?*   Now that you have explored how the Speed Tests can be applied to your business let's return to that question again. In particular, to quantify the potential impact (%) on your organization's growth of the goals you set out in relation to the Speed Tests above. Let's do this in three steps:

Step 1: Put the percentage of your organization's growth potential being exploited today on the scale below. You might like to refer back to how you answered this question on page one of this book.

> *Q: What percentage of your company's full growth potential is presently being exploited? Circle the point on the scale below.*

0%   10%   20%   30%   40%   50%   60%   70%   80%   90%   100%
(% of full growth potential exploited)

Step 2: Create a summary view of the Speed Tests you have selected (earlier) and their potential impact in the diagram below:

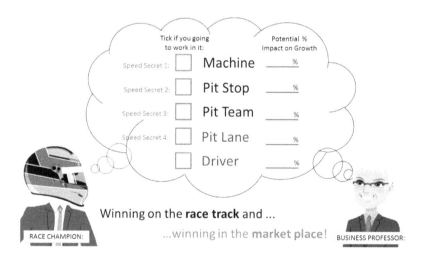

Step 3: Add up the impact of all the areas that you have selected to work on (ticked in the diagram above) to estimate the combined impact

in terms of increasing the percentage of your organization's growth potential being exploited.

Q: What percentage of your company's full growth potential would be exploited if you worked on the above Speed Tests over the next 12 months? Circle the point on the scale below.

0%	10%	20%	30%	40%	50%	60%	70%	90%	100%

(% of full growth potential exploited)

With your goal now set it is time to accelerate. Here is hoping you enjoy the thrill of going faster. We look forward to seeing you and your team on the winner's podium. Let's leave the last words to the most successful F1™ racer ever and the man to which this book is dedicated. We began this book with this quote, but because it so perfectly conveys the performance ethos of F1™, let's use it to close:

> *My philosophy is never to think you have achieved it! Always looking for the millimeters/seconds ... find it on lap 50 of the third day!*
> Michael Schumacher[280]

APPENDICES

- Run Your Own Pitstop

- Predictive Growth Analytics

- Growth Psychology

- About the Authors

- Books in the Series

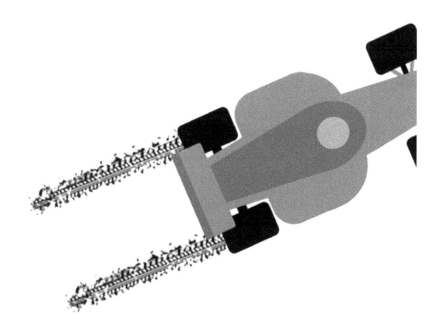

RUN YOUR OWN PITSTOP

Want to run your own Growth Pitstop™? Now you can get everything you need delivered in a box.

The Growth Pitstop™ combines the latest research and analysis into strategy, growth and innovation with exercises that are metric driven, challenging and high energy. It is ideal for conferences, away-days, planning workshops and team-building events.

Whether you are a manager, an in-house trainer, or an external consultant, or coach the Growth Pitstop™ kit contains everything you need to run a powerful management team workshop. It includes;

- Starting Grid poster and stickers (A1 size)
- Formula for Growth™ floor jig-saw (16 A3 pieces)
- Action Tracker (A1 size)
- Instructions, plus links to video and other materials
- Formula for Growth™ books for your team

Visit **www.growthpitstop.com** for information or to order.

PREDICTIVE GROWTH ANALYTICS

Want an assessment of your organization, business unit, or team's growth performance and potential? The Growth Pitstop® is the fastest and most powerful way.

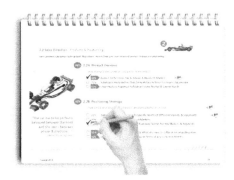

In high speed racing, a rapid assessment of performance and potential is key. Business is no different. The online Growth Pitstop® assessment is used by senior management teams to:

- Create their own Growth Potential Index Score & benchmark
- Engage cross functional stakeholder perspectives on growth
- Accelerate the process of data gathering
- Identify hidden growth potential
- Highlight potential risks
- Save time and prevent analysis paralysis
- Validate/test PitStop decision making with data analytics.

The online assessment measures 248 growth-related variables that are proven predictors of growth. Then sophisticated algorithms and visualization tools analyse, benchmark and present organization, unit or team results in a powerful 50 page report. To request access to the diagnostic visit: **www.growthpitstop.com**.

> *The Growth PitStop team report format is the most visually appealing and action orientated on the market today.*
> Deiric McCann, Profiles International

THE PSYCHOLOGY OF GROWTH

The Ultimate
Speed-o-meter Is:

Inside The
Executive's
Head

There is a psychology to growth. That is to say what goes on in the heads of mangers and their teams really matters. For this reason, the Growth Pitstop™ employs the latest insights into how people engage with complex issues, how people learn and the process of changing attitudes and behaviors.

To enable managers to find more effective solutions to today's increasingly complex business problems, the Growth Pitstop™ leverages a range of powerful techniques, including:

• Change Modelling – a six-step change model based on the latest research into the requirements of successful and sustained change.

• Cognitive Re-framing – to enable people to engage with the subject of growth performance in a way that is free of personalities and politics.

• Mental Modelling – it engages with and indeed challenges traditional modes of thinking; that is people's dominant mental models when it comes to business development, strategy and growth.

• Systems Thinking – helping managers to see inter-relationships and linkages that may have been previously overlooked.

• Results-Based Learning – engaging individuals and teams in solving their own problems as a means of accelerating learning and building engagement / commitment.

As far as we are aware the Growth Pitstop® is the first model that blends these techniques together.

ABOUT THE AUTHORS

This book is the joint creation of 2750 managers across 12 industries. Its ideas and insights emerged workshop by workshop and assessment by assessment over a period of 9 years thanks to managers from organizations, such as; IBM, BT, 3M, ARUP and Medtronics. As there are too many people to name, it is the names of Ray Collis (Oslo) and John O Gorman (Dublin) - who put into words and paragraphs the wisdom of these managers - that appear on the cover.

Ray and John bring Formula One™ principles of performance, including teamwork, data analytics and innovation, to cross functional management teams. They combine the passion for winning from F1™ with cutting edge business research and analytics to unlock hidden growth potential of 7-25% within organizations and teams.

John O Gorman lives in Dublin (Ireland) and is an executive coach in business performance. His passion is performance psychology, unlocking human potential and aligning models of growth. He uses the Growth Pitstop® to support the design and development of growth programmes for organizations and teams across Europe. John holds an international MBA, Bachelor of Commerce Degree and Diplomas in Marketing and Executive Coaching.

Ray Collis lives in Oslo (Norway) and brings the numbers and strategy dimension to the Growth Pitstop®'s science and psychology equation. He led the development of the Growth Pitstop®'s online data analytics and algorithm. These have been used across 47 countries to identify hidden growth potential of 7% - 25% with speed and accuracy for firms across the financial services, pharmaceutical, medical device and high tech sectors. Ray holds a

Master Degree in Business, Bachelor of Commerce and accreditations in strategy, sales, marketing and research.

John, Ray and their growing network of Growth Pitstop® partners work with several Fortune 1000 organizations, with five of their clients ranked in the top 3 firms in their sectors globally. All of these clients share a similar goal "unlocking sustainable growth potential". They are constantly looking for opportunities to accelerate leaders, organizations and teams. To contact John and Ray or their team please email: **support@growthpitstop.com.**

OTHER BOOKS IN THE SERIES

The 'Growth Pitstop™' is part of a series of four books. There is an overview of the other books in the series presented here.

FORMULA FOR GROWTH™

The 'Formula for Growth™' provides access to more of the research that underpins the Growth Pitstop™ approach. It looks at your organization, business unit or team as a revenue generating machine - akin to fast race car. Packed with insights, benchmarking data and practical tools it examines the key requirements of accelerating sustained and profitable growth, including:

- Focused Ambition (Priorities, Resources & Commitment)
- Market Targeting (Customers, Competitors & Channels)
- Product Traction (Products, Messages & Positioning)
- Visibility & Control (Systems, Structures, Reporting & Compliance)
- Customer Acquisition (Sales & Marketing) & Retention (Account Management, Service & Support)
- Driver & Team (Leadership, Motivation and Skills)

Format:	Hardback	ISBN:	978-1-907725-04-3
Pages:	609	Date:	July 2016

THE REVENUE TRACK™

'The Revenue Track™' links strategy (the stuff of The Growth Pitstop™) with implementation to tackle the execution challenge. Continuing the racing theme, it takes your growth machine onto the track (or into the marketplace) to execute its strategy for growth. It explores the cross-functional capabilities, processes and systems that underpin the acquisition and retention of customers.

Format:	Hardback (full color)	ISBN:	978-1-907725-03-6
Pages:	500	Date:	Oct. 2016

THE B2B SALES REVOLUTION™

'The B2B Sales Revolution' reveals the new complexity of corporate buying and presents a compendium of best practice buyer-friendly tools to be used in the acquisition and retention of customers at each stage of the Revenue Track™.

Format:	Hardback	ISBN:	978-1-907725-00-5
Pages:	347	Date:	2010

BIBLIOGRAPHY

1 Jean Alesi, French racing driver, quoted on BrainyQuote. Link: http://www.brainyquote.com/quotes/quotes/j/jeanalesi331976.html

2 Michael Schumacher interviewed by Jonathan Noble in 2002 related in Daly, D. 'Race to Win: How to Become a Complete Champion Driver,' Motorbooks, 2008.

3 Dale Earnhardt American former race car driver and team owner. Quoted on Brainyquote. Link: http://www.brainyquote.com/quotes/authors/d/dale_earnhardt.

4 Michael Schumacher – a Formula One™ legend and winner of 7 Championships – source 'Quotes from Formula 1' Link: http://f1quotes.tumblr.com/post/34167189201

5 John P. Kotter, 'Accelerate: Building Strategic Agility for a Faster-Moving World,' Harvard Business Review Press, 2014.

6 Daly, D. 'Race to Win: How to Become a Complete Champion Driver,' Motorbooks, 2008.

7 Bain & Company research explores the ability of organizations to meet the 5.5% challenge. This is examined in Section 1: Need for Speed in the context of 'triple acceleration'.

8 Quote from F1Quotes at: http://f1quotes.tumblr.com/post/37787046321/life-is-all-about-challenges-and-most-important

9 Hermann Tilke is German engineer, auto racer and F1™ race circuit designer. Quote from 'Quotes from Formula 1' link: http://f1quotes.tumblr.com/.

10 Tim Jones, Dave McCormick & Caroline Dewing, 'Growth Champions: The Battle for Sustained Innovation Leadership (Growth Agenda)', John Wiley & Sons, Mar 2012.

11 Frank V. Cespedes, 'Aligning Strategy and Sales: The Choices, Systems, and Behaviors that Drive Effective Selling,' HBR Press, 2014

12 Robert Bloom & Dave Conti, 'The Inside Advantage: The Strategy that Unlocks the Hidden Growth in Your Business', McGraw-Hill Education, 2007.

13 Sean Ellis & Morgan Brown, 'Startup Growth Engines: Case Studies of How Today's Most Successful Startups Unlock Extraordinary Growth', Ellis & Brown, 2014.

14 Rupert Merson, 'Growing a Business: Strategies for leaders and entrepreneurs' Economist Books, 2016.

15 Garry Hammel, 'What Matters Now: How to win in a world of relentless change…'Jossey-Boss, 2012.

16 The 'pick a vehicle' exercise is a 'Projective Technique' – that is a psychological test which enable 'subjects to project their own personalities into the test… often revealing personal conflicts, motivations, coping styles, and other characteristics'.
Read more: Projective Techniques - Test, Tests, Subjects, and Rorschach - JRank Articles:
http://psychology.jrank.org/pages/506/Projective-Techniques.html

17 Roger Martin, the dean of Rothman School of Management quoted in Christian Madsbjerg & Mikkel B. Rasmussen, 'The Moment of Clarity: Using the Human Sciences to Solve Your Toughest Business Problems', Harvard Business Review Press, 2014.

18 Chris Zook and James Allen, 'Repeatability,' HBR Press, 2012.

19 Chris Zook and James Allen, 'Repeatability,' HBR Press, 2012.

[20] Garry Hammel, Foreward to 'Beyond Performance: How Great Organizations Build Ultimate Competitive Advantage', Scott Keller & Colin Price, Wiley 2011.

21 Chris Zook, 'Beyond the Core: Expand Your Market Without Abandoning Your Roots' Harvard Business Review Press, 2004.

22 Thomas Baumgartner, Homayoun Hatami, et al, 'Sales Growth: Five Proven Strategies from the World's Sales Leaders', John Wiley & Sons, May 2012.

23 Deloitte Shift Index, 2013.

24 Dating from 1957 the Ansoff Matrix is the creation of Igor Ansoff. It is a strategic planning tool to help executives and marketers devise strategies for future growth. For more info: https://en.wikipedia.org/wiki/Ansoff_Matrix

25 Patrick Viguerie, Sven Smit & Mehrdad Baghai, 'The Granularity of Growth: How to Identify the Sources of Growth and Drive Enduring Company Performance', Marshall Cavendish, 2008.

26 Larry Bossidy, Ram Charan & Charles Burck, 'Execution: The Discipline of Getting Things Done (Updated)', Random House Business Books, 2011.

27 Charles O'Reilly & Michael Tushman, 'Ambidexterity as a Dynamic Capability: Resolving the Innovator's Dilemma', Working Paper, Stanford Graduate School of Business, March 2007

28 Towers Watson Inc., '2013 Change and Communication ROI Study -What Change Leaders Need to Get Right'Link: https://www.towerswatson.com/en/Insights/IC-Types/Survey-Research-Results/2013/08/Infographic-2-2013-Change-and-Communication-ROI-Study

29 James A. Belasco, 'Teaching the Elephant to Dance', Crown 1991.

30 Richard P. Rumelt, 'Good/Bad Strategy,' Profile Books, 2012.

31 Larry E. Greiner, 'Evolution and Revolution as Organizations Grow'. HBR May-June 1998. Link: https://hbr.org/1998/05/evolution-and-revolution-as-organizations-grow

32 Christian Madsbjerg & Mikkel B. Rasmussen, 'The Moment of Clarity: Using the Human Sciences to Solve Your Toughest Business Problems', Harvard Business Review Press, 2014.

33 Criteria for inclusion in the Deloite Technology Fast 500™ for North America 2015. Criteria for inclusion: Must own proprietary intellectual property/technology, current year operating revenues of at least $5m and in business a minimum of 4 years. See Fast 500 list at: http://www2.deloitte.com/content/dam/Deloitte/us/Documents/technology-media-telecommunications/Technology-Fast-500-Winners-Ranking-List.pdf. Analysis of Fast 500 for 2015 from Deloitte Infographic: http://www2.deloitte.com/content/dam/Deloitte/us/Images/Misc/Infographics/Technology-Fast-500-Infographic.pdf

34 Dr. Kirsti Dautzenberg, Study on Fast Growing Young Companies (Gazelles) - Summary, On behalf of the Bundesministerium für Wirtschaft und Technologie, June 2012. Link: https://www.bmwi.de/BMWi/Redaktion/PDF/Publikationen/Studien/studie-ueber-schnell-wachsende-jungunternehmen-gazellen-kurzfassung-en,property=pdf,bereich=bmwi2012,sprache=de,rwb=true.pdf

35 What we call 'Fit for F1™' has often been called a Gazelle - that is a high-growth company that more than doubles its revenue over a four-year period (20%+ per annum), starting from a revenue base of at least $1 million.   Although the stereotype of a fast growth company is of the young hi-tech company, they can come from all sectors, sizes and age groups. What they all have in common is their importance for economic prosperity.

36 Robert E. Litan (vice president of Research and Policy at the Kauffman Foundation) quoted in 'High-Growth Gazelle Companies Account for 10 Percent of New Jobs' by Rieva Lesonsky on Smallbiztrends.com, Mar 9th 2010. Link: http://smallbiztrends.com/2010/05/high-growth-gazelle-companies-10-percent-new-jobs.html

37 Chris Zook, 'Beyond the Core: Expand Your Market Without Abandoning Your Roots' Harvard Business Review Press, 2004.

38 John P. Kotter, 'XLR8 Accelerate: Building Strategic Agility for a Faster-Moving World,' Harvard Business Review Press, 2014.

39 John P. Kotter, 'Accelerate: Building Strategic Agility for a Faster-Moving World,' Harvard Business Review Press, 2014.

40 Martin Reeves, Knut Haanaes & Janmejaya Sinha, 'Your Strategy Needs a Strategy: How to Choose and Execute the Right Approach', Harvard Business Review Press (19 May 2015)

41 John P. Kotter, 'Accelerate: Building Strategic Agility for a Faster-Moving World,' Harvard Business Review Press, 2014.

42 Clayton Christensen, 'The Innovator's Dilemma: When New Technologies Cause Great Firms to Fail (Management of Innovation and Change)', Harvard Business Review Press, 2015.

43 A great example of the use of the racetrack as a metaphor for accelerating new growth opportunities is John P. Kotter's, 'Accelerate: Building Strategic Agility for a Faster-Moving World,' Harvard Business Review Press, 2014.

44 Rita Gunther McGrath & Ian C. Macmillan, 'Discovery-Driven Growth: A Breakthrough Process to Reduce Risk and Seize Opportunity', Harvard Business Review Press, 2009.

45 Rowan Gibson, 'The Four Lenses of Innovation: A Power Tool for Creative Thinking,' April 2015.

46 Oliver Gassmann, Karolin Frankenberger & Michaela Csik, 'The Business Model Navigator: 55 Models That Will Revolutionise Your Business', FT Press, 2015.

47 Scott Keller & Colin Price, 'Beyond Performance: How Great Organizations Build Ultimate Competitive Advantage', Wiley 2011.

48 Donald Sull, 'The Upside of Turbulence: Seizing Opportunity in an Uncertain World,' HarperBusiness, 2009.

49 Rowan Gibson, 'The Four Lenses of Innovation: A Power Tool for Creative Thinking,' April 2015.

50 Anne Miller, 'Metaphorically Selling: How to Use the Magic of Metaphors to Sell, Persuade, and Explain Anything to Anyone,' 2004

51 Christian Madsbjerg & Mikkel B. Rasmussen, 'The Moment of Clarity: Using the Human Sciences to Solve Your Toughest Business Problems', Harvard Business Review Press, 2014.

52 Frank Cespedes, 'Aligning Strategy and Sales,' HBR Press, 2014.

53 Mark Gottfredson, 'The Breakthrough Imperative: How the Best Managers Get Outstanding Results', HarperBusiness, 2011.

54 Lakoff & Johnson, 'Metaphors We Live By,' University of Chicago Press, 1981

55 Lakoff & Johnson, 'Metaphors We Live By,' University of Chicago Press, 1981

56 Peter M. Senge, 'The Fifth Discipline: The Art and Practice of The Learning Organization,' Doubleday; Revised and Updated edition, 2006.

57 Wendy Sullivan & Judy Rees, 'Clean Language,' 'Revealing Metaphors and Opening Minds,' Crown House Publishing, 2012.

58 Sarah Passmore, Jonathan Cantore & Stefan Lewis, Appreciative Inquiry for Change Management: Using AI to Facilitate Organizational Development: Volume 1, Kogan Page, 2011.

59 Juanita Brown, David Isaacs, et al., 'The World Café: Shaping Our Futures Through Conversations That Matter', Berrett-Koehler Publishers, 2005.

60 Psychologists tell us that the drive to maintain a consistency between our inner world (what goes on in our heads) and the outer world (or reality) is very strong. One implication is that it can be hard for us to act in a manner inconsistent with our internal narrative. That is not to say that people are not capable of saying one thing and doing something entirely different. Or that we cannot be duplicitous or deceiving in our words or actions. Far from it. What we are saying is that it is hard for us to act in consistent with how we see things in our own heads – that our internal narrative rules supreme.

61 Yoram Wind and Colin Crooke, 'Making Better Sense: How Your Mental Models Define Your World', FT Press, 2010.

62 Christian Madsbjerg & Mikkel B. Rasmussen, 'The Moment of Clarity: Using the Human Sciences to Solve Your Toughest Business Problems', Harvard Business Review Press, 2014.

63 Jean Alesi was a driver for the Ferrari team in the 1990s. Quote from 'Quotes from Formula 1'. Link: http://f1quotes.tumblr.com/post/39214578364/you-tend-to-think-that-there-is-a-big-gap-between

64 Cognitive re-framing is 'to change the conceptual and/or emotional setting or viewpoint from which a situation is experienced and to place it in another frame which fits the 'facts' equally well or even better, and thereby changing its entire meaning' according to Watzlawick, P., Weakland, J. and Fisch, R., 'Change: Principles of Problem Formation and Problem Resolution,' NY: Norton, 1974.

65 Chris Ertel & Lisa Kay Solomon, 'Moments of Impact: How to Design Strategic Conversations That Accelerate Change,' 2014.

66 'Creative Destruction Whips Corporate America', Innosight Executive Briefing, Winter 2012.

67 John P. Kotter, 'Accelerate: Building Strategic Agility for a Faster-Moving World,' Harvard Business Review Press, 2014.

68 Rupert Merson, 'Growing a Business: Strategies for leaders and entrepreneurs' Economist Books, 2016.

69 Mark Gottfredson, 'The Breakthrough Imperative: How the Best Managers Get Outstanding Results', HarperBusiness, 2011.

70 James Kerr, 'Legacy', Little Brown Book Group, 2013.

71 Oliver Gassmann, Karolin Frankenberger & Michaela Csik, 'The Business Model Navigator: 55 Models That Will Revolutionise Your Business', FT Press, 2015.

72 Warren Berger, 'A More Beautiful Question: The Power of Inquiry to Spark Breakthrough Ideas', Bloomsbury, 2014.

73 Clayton Christensen, 'The Innovator's Dilemma: When New Technologies Cause Great Firms to Fail (Management of Innovation and Change)', Harvard Business Review Press, 2015.

74 Carol Dweck, 'Mindset: The New Psychology of Success', Ballantine Books, 2007

75 Ralph L. Kliem, Creative, Efficient, and Effective Project Management, 2013, ISBN-10: 1466576928

76 Rowan Gibson, 'The Four Lenses of Innovation: A Power Tool for Creative Thinking,' April 2015.

77 Rowan Gibson, 'The Four Lenses of Innovation: A Power Tool for Creative Thinking,' April 2015.

78 Christian Madsbjerg & Mikkel B. Rasmussen, 'The Moment of Clarity: Using the Human Sciences to Solve Your Toughest Business Problems', Harvard Business Review Press, 2014.

79 Mark Jenkins, Ken Pasternak, Richard West, 'Performance at the Limit: Business Lessons from Formula 1® Motor Racing', Cambridge University Press; 3 edition (2 Jun. 2016).

80 Robert I. Sutton & Huggy Rao, 'Scaling Up Excellence: Getting to More Without Settling for Less', Crown Business; 2014.

81 Bernie Ecclestone quoted in Wikipedia.
Link: https://en.wikipedia.org/wiki/107%25_rule

82 Mario Andretti retired Italian-American world champion racing driver quoted on BrainyQuote:
http://www.brainyquote.com/quotes/quotes/m/marioandre636602.html

83 Christian Madsbjerg & Mikkel B. Rasmussen, 'The Moment of Clarity: Using the Human Sciences to Solve Your Toughest Business Problems', Harvard Business Review Press, 2014.

84 Sean Ellis & Morgan Brown, 'Startup Growth Engines: Case Studies of How Today's Most Successful Startups Unlock Extraordinary Growth', Ellis & Brown, 2014.

85 Christopher Ryan, Nate Warren & Gail Carson, 'Winning B2B Marketing: Proven Methods that Drive Revenue, Leads and Awareness', Fusion Marketing Press (May 1, 2014)

86 Neil Rackham in the forward to 'Rethinking Sales Management: A Strategic Guide for Practitioners' by Beth Rogers, John Wiley & Sons, Aug 2007.

87 J.-C. Spender & Bruce A. Strong, 'Strategic Conversations: Creating and Directing the Entrepreneurial Workforce,' Cambridge University Press, 2014.

88 Chris Ertel & Lisa Kay Solomon, 'Moments of Impact: How to Design Strategic Conversations That Accelerate Change,' 2014.

89 Richard P. Rumelt, 'Good/Bad Strategy,' Profile Books, 2012.

90 Albert Einstein quote from AZ Quotes. Link:
http://www.azquotes.com/quote/702499

91 J.-C. Spender & Bruce A. Strong, 'Strategic Conversations: Creating and Directing the Entrepreneurial Workforce,' Cambridge University Press, 2014.

92 Chris Ertel & Lisa Kay Solomon, 'Moments of Impact: How to Design Strategic Conversations That Accelerate Change,' 2014.

93 Chris Ertel & Lisa Kay Solomon, 'Moments of Impact: How to Design Strategic Conversations That Accelerate Change,' 2014.

94 Tom Peters, 'A Brief History of the 7-S ("McKinsey 7-S") Model'. Link: http://tompeters.com/docs/7SHistory.pdf

95 Anne-Christine Cadiat, 'McKinsey 7S Framework: Understand the connections within your business', 50MINUTES.COM, 2015.

96 Kees van der Heijden, 'Scenarios, The Art of Strategic Conversation', Wiley, 2005.

97 Buckminster Fuller quoted in 'The Fifth Discipline', Peter M. Senge, Doubleday 2006.

98 Scott Keller & Colin Price, 'Beyond Performance: How Great Organizations Build Ultimate Competitive Advantage', Wiley 2011.

99 Scott Keller & Colin Price, 'Beyond Performance: How Great Organizations Build Ultimate Competitive Advantage', Wiley 2011.

100 Sydney Finkelstein, 'Superbosses: How Exceptional Leaders Master the Flow of Talent', Portfolio, 2016.

101 John Seely Brown quoted in 'ReModel: Create mental models to improve your life and lead simply and effectively' by Joshua Spodek, Kindle Edition.

102 Tim Jones, Dave McCormick & Caroline Dewing, 'Growth Champions: The Battle for Sustained Innovation Leadership (Growth Agenda)', John Wiley & Sons, Mar 2012.

103 Donald C. Hambrick and James W. Fredrickson, 'Are you sure you have a strategy?', Academy of Management Executive, 2005, Vol. 19, No. 4

104 Robert Peters, 'Growth Hacking Techniques, Disruptive Technology - How 40 Companies Made It BIG - Online Growth Hacker Marketing Strategy', World Ideas, 2014

105 Michael Gerber, 'The E Myth Revisited: Why Most Small Businesses Don't Work and What to Do About It', HarperCollins, 1995.

106 J.-C. Spender, 'Business Strategy: Managing Uncertainty, Opportunity, and Enterprise', Oxford University Press, 2014.

107 Arie Geus, 'The Living Company: Growth, Learning and Longevity in Business', Nicholas Brealey Publishing, 2011.

108 Neil Roberts, 'Think Fast: The Racer's Why-To Guide to Winning,' CreateSpace , 2010.

109 Patrick M. Lencioni, 'The Advantage: Why Organizational Health Trumps Everything Else In Business,' Jossey-Bass, 2012.

110 Tom Peters, 'A Brief History of the 7-S ("McKinsey 7-S") Model'. Link: http://tompeters.com/docs/7SHistory.pdf

111 Sarah Passmore, Jonathan Cantore & Stefan Lewis, Appreciative Inquiry for Change Management: Using AI to Facilitate Organizational Development: Volume 1, Kogan Page, 2011.

112 Chris Ertel & Lisa Kay Solomon, 'Moments of Impact: How to Design Strategic Conversations That Accelerate Change,' 2014.

113 A.G. Lafley & Roger L. Martin, 'Playing to Win: How Strategy Really Works,' HBR Press, 2013.

114 Yoram Wind and Colin Crooke, 'Making Better Sense: How Your Mental Models Define Your World', FT Press, 2010.

115 Cynthia Montgomery, 'The Strategist: Be the Leader Your Business Needs,' HarperBusiness, 2012.

116 Neil Roberts, 'Think Fast: The Racer's Why-To Guide to Winning,' CreateSpace , 2010.

117 Legendary race commentator Murray Walker quoted on BrainyQuote.

118 Kees van der Heijden, 'Scenarios: The Art of Strategic Conversation,' Wiley, 2011.

119 The Physics Hypertextbook, Equations of Motion. Link: http://physics.info/motion-equations/

120 Martin Reeves, Knut Haanaes & Janmejaya Sinha, 'Your Strategy Needs a Strategy: How to Choose and Execute the Right Approach', Harvard Business Review Press (19 May 2015)

121 The Physics Hypertextbook, Equations of Motion. Link:
http://physics.info/motion-equations/

122 '20 Things You Didn't KNow about Enzo Ferrari',
on Supercompressor.com, by Aaron Muller and Ted Gushue, 5/8/14. Link:
http://www.supercompressor.com/rides/20-enzo-ferrari-facts-that-you-
might-not-know

123 Quote attributed to the late French racer Jean-Pierre Beltoise. For more
on JPB: https://en.wikipedia.org/wiki/Jean-Pierre_Beltoise.

124 Ken Favaro, Kasturi Rangan, et al, 'The Executive Guide to Strategy,' PwC
Strategy& LLC, 2013.

125 A.G. Lafley & Roger L. Martin, 'Playing to Win: How Strategy Really
Works,' HBR Press, 2013.

126 Jeroen De Flander, 'The Execution Shortcut: Why Some Strategies Take
the Hidden Path to Success and Others Never Reach the Finish Line', the
performance factory, 2013.

127 George Labovitz & Victor Rosansky, 'The Power of Alignment: How Great
Companies Stay Centered and Accomplish Extraordinary Things', Wiley 2008.

128 Frank V. Cespedes, 'Aligning Strategy and Sales: The Choices, Systems,
and Behaviors that Drive Effective Selling,' HBR Press, 2014.

129 Frank V. Cespedes, 'Aligning Strategy and Sales: The Choices, Systems,
and Behaviors that Drive Effective Selling,' HBR Press, 2014

130 Paul Leinwand & Cesare R. Mainardi, 'Strategy That Works: How Winning
Companies Close the Strategy-to-Execution Gap', Harvard Business Review
Press, 2016.

131 Gallagher, M., 'The Business of Winning: Strategic Success from the Formula One™
Track to the Boardroom,' Kogan Page, 2014.

132 Tom Peters, 'Thriving on Chaos: Handbook for a Management Revolution',
Harper Perennial, 1988.

133 Richard D'Aveni, 'Hyper-competition - Managing the Dynamics of Strategic Maneuvering', 1994

134 Ray Kurzweil, Perspectives on Business Innovation. Published on KurzweilAI.net May 1, 2003.

135 Ray Kurzweil, Perspectives on Business Innovation. Published on KurzweilAI.net May 1, 2003.

136 Martin Reeves, Knut Haanaes & Janmejaya Sinha, 'Your Strategy Needs a Strategy: How to Choose and Execute the Right Approach', Harvard Business Review Press (19 May 2015)

137 Colin McRae , late Scottish champion rally driver, quote from AZ Quotes. Link: http://www.azquotes.com/quote/780950

138 Garry Hammel, 'What Matters Now: How to win in a world of relentless change...'Jossey-Boss, 2012.

139 Donald Sull, 'The Upside of Turbulence: Seizing Opportunity in an Uncertain World,' HarperBusiness, 2009.

140 IBM CEO Survey 2010.

141 Tom Peters, Re-imagine, Dorling Kindersley, 2004.

142 Jayne May & Charles May, 'Are you VUCA ready?,' CreateSpace, 2014.

143 F1™ racing champion Mario Andretti quote from: http://justacarguy.blogspot.ie/2010/08/best-quotes-and-sayings-about-car.html

144 Reeves, Love & Mathur, BCG Report: 'The Most Adaptive Companies 2012, Winning in an Age of Turbulence'

145 Ronald Cohen, 'The Second Bounce Of The Ball: Turning Risk Into Opportunity', Weidenfeld & Nicolson, 2010.

146 Martin Reeves, Knut Haanaes & Janmejaya Sinha, 'Your Strategy Needs a Strategy: How to Choose and Execute the Right Approach', Harvard Business Review Press (19 May 2015)

147 Chris Zook, 'Unstoppable: Finding Hidden Assets to Renew the Core and Fuel Profitable Growth,' Harvard Business Review Press, 2007.

148 Rita Gunther McGrath & Ian C. Macmillan, 'Discovery-Driven Growth: A Breakthrough Process to Reduce Risk and Seize Opportunity', Harvard Business Review Press, 2009.

149 The failure statistics for traditional strategy are widely used and remarkably consistent. See for example 'The Fractal Organization: Creating sustainable organizations...' By Patrick Hoverstadt and Richard P. Rumelt's 'Good Strategy/Bad Strategy'.

150 Yves Morieux and Peter Tollman, in their book '6 Simple Rules', Harvard Business Review Press, 2014.

151 Kees van der Heijden, 'Scenarios, The Art of Strategic Conversation', Wiley, 2005.

152 John P. Kotter, 'Accelerate: Building Strategic Agility for a Faster-Moving World,' Harvard Business Review Press, 2014.

153 Chris Zook and James Allen, 'Repeatability,' HBR Press, 2012

154 Charles O'Reilly & Michael Tushman, 'Ambidexterity as a Dynamic Capability: Resolving the Innovator's Dilemma', Working Paper, Stanford Graduate School of Business, March 2007

155 Henry Mintzberg, 'The Fall and Rise of Strategic Planning', HBR Jan-Feb, 2014.

156 Patrick Hoverstadt, 'The Fractal Organization: Creating sustainable Organizations,' Wiley, 2009.

157 Martin Reeves, Knut Haanaes & Janmejaya Sinha, 'Your Strategy Needs a Strategy: How to Choose and Execute the Right Approach', Harvard Business Review Press, 2015.

158 The challenge of performance management is evident from the following studies:
- In a Deloitte survey more than half of executives said that their organization's approach to performance management neither drives employee engagement or high performance. Quotes in Martin Reeves, Knut Haanaes & Janmejaya Sinha, 'Your Strategy Needs a Strategy: How to Choose

and Execute the Right Approach', Harvard Business Review Press, 2015.
- According to Mercer's 2013 Global Performance Management Survey
Report, managers struggle in particular to: have candid performance dialog
(33%) and to link performance to development planning (48%), providing
career development coaching and direction (59%) – figures shown indicate
percentage rating skills as 'marginal' in each area. Link:
http://www.mercer.com/content/dam/mercer/attachments/global/Talent/As
sess-BrochurePerfMgmt.pdf

159 The pit team works on the car and the driver together, they are not seen
in isolation. Yet, the performance debate for most managers tends to focus
solely on the driver in the cockpit – something which the Formula for
Growth™ with its broader view of the many drivers of success is aimed at
avoiding.

160 Marcus Buckingham & Ashley Goodall, 'Reinventing Performance
Management', HBR, Apr. 2015. Link: https://hbr.org/2015/04/reinventing-
performance-management

161 'Why The Annual Performance Review Is Going Extinct' By Kris Duggan on
FastCompany.com.
Link: http://www.fastcompany.com/3052135/the-future-of-work/why-the-
annual-performance-review-is-going-extinct).

162 'Why The Annual Performance Review Is Going Extinct' By Kris Duggan on
FastCompany.com.
Link: http://www.fastcompany.com/3052135/the-future-of-work/why-the-
annual-performance-review-is-going-extinct)

163 Jim Highsmith's book 'Agile Software Development Ecosystems' quoted in
"Where is the Proof That Agile Methods Work?" by Scott W.
Ambler (Ambysoft Inc). Link:
http://www.agilemodeling.com/essays/proof.htm

164 Reeves, Love & Mathur, 'The Most Adaptive Companies 2012, Winning in
an Age of Turbulence', BCG Report 2012.

165 Robert Kegan & Lisa Laskow Lahey, 'Immunity to Change: How to
Overcome It and Unlock the Potential in Yourself and Your Organization',
Harvard Business Review Press, 2009.

166 Richard P. Rumelt, 'Good/Bad Strategy,' Profile Books, 2012.

167 Sean Ellis & Morgan Brown, 'Startup Growth Engines: Case Studies of How Today's Most Successful Startups Unlock Extraordinary Growth', Ellis & Brown, 2014.

168 Kees van der Heijden, 'Scenarios, The Art of Strategic Conversation', Wiley, 2005.

169 Bill Walsh, Steve Jamison & Craig Walsh, 'The Score Takes Care of Itself: My Philosophy of Leadership', Penguin Publishing Group, 2009.

170 Reeves & Haanaes, 'Your Strategy Needs a Strategy', Harvard Business Review Press, 2015.

171 Rupert Merson, 'Growing a Business: Strategies for leaders and entrepreneurs' Economist Books, 2016.

172 Donald Sull, 'The Upside of Turbulence: Seizing Opportunity in an Uncertain World,' HarperBusiness, 2009.

173 Kees van der Heijden, 'Scenarios, The Art of Strategic Conversation', Wiley, 2005.

174 Richard P. Rumelt, 'Good/Bad Strategy,' Profile Books, 2012.

175 Patrick Thean, 'Rhythm: How to Achieve Breakthrough Execution and Accelerate Growth,' Greenleaf Book Group, 2014.

176 A team based, as well as bottom-up, approach to strategy and execution is a cornerstone of contemporary business thinking. In the old model of the strategist (a senior manager or consultant) thinks on behalf of the entire organization. He or she works out an optimal strategy and hands it over to others for implementation.

177 Research consistently shows that Collaborative learning is more than twice as effective as Individual learning measured in terms of academic achievement, self-esteem and so on. See MICHAEL PRINCE, 'Does Active Learning Work?' A Review of the Research, Journal of Engineering Education, 93(3), 2004.

178 IBM Design Thinking Principles – 'a framework for teaming and action'. Link: http://www.ibm.com/design/thinking/

179 Most recently this research has focused on the ability to have strategic conversations as key to success, but this is just the latest in a long line of research under headings that include; organizational health, organizational learning, change management, action learning and appreciative inquiry.

180 Gallagher, M., 'The Business of Winning: Strategic Success from the Formula One™ Track to the Boardroom,' Kogan Page, 2014.

181 Dave Barry is an award winning American author. Quote from BrainQuote. Link: http://www.brainyquote.com/quotes/quotes/d/davebarry102229.html

182 Mark de Rond & Richard Hytner, 'There Is an I in Team: What Elite Athletes and Coaches Really Know About High Performance', Harvard Business Review Press, 2012.

183 Mark de Rond & Richard Hytner, 'There Is an I in Team: What Elite Athletes and Coaches Really Know About High Performance', Harvard Business Review Press, 2012.

184 IBM Design Thinking Principles – 'a framework for teaming and action'. Link: http://www.ibm.com/design/thinking/

185 'Understanding F1™ Racing – Pitstops' on formula1.com Link: https://www.formula1.com/content/fom-website/en/championship/inside-f1/understanding-f1-racing/Pit_stops.html

186 Chris Ertel & Lisa Kay Solomon, 'Moments of Impact: How to Design Strategic Conversations That Accelerate Change,' 2014.

187 Larry Bossidy, Ram Charan & Charles Burck, 'Execution: The Discipline of Getting Things Done,' Crown Business, 2002.

188 Chris Ertel & Lisa Kay Solomon, 'Moments of Impact: How to Design Strategic Conversations That Accelerate Change,' 2014.

189 This rough calculation is based on an average burdened salary figure of $130,000. That is salary plus related costs, such as insurance and overhead.

190 Towers Watson, "2009/2010 Communication ROI Study Report: Capitalizing on Effective Communication," Link: https://www.towerswatson.com/en/Insights/IC-Types/Survey-Research-

Results/2009/12/20092010-Communication-ROI-Study-Report-Capitalizing-on-Effective-Communication

191 Chris Ertel & Lisa Kay Solomon, 'Moments of Impact: How to Design Strategic Conversations That Accelerate Change,' 2014.

192 J.-C. Spender & Bruce A. Strong, 'Strategic Conversations: Creating and Directing the Entrepreneurial Workforce,' Cambridge University Press, 2014.

193 Gordon Curphy & Robert Hogan, 'The Rocket Model: Practical Advice for Building High Performing Teams,' Hogan Press, 2012.

194 Chris Ertel & Lisa Kay Solomon, 'Moments of Impact: How to Design Strategic Conversations That Accelerate Change,' 2014.

195 J.-C. Spender & Bruce A. Strong, 'Strategic Conversations: Creating and Directing the Entrepreneurial Workforce,' Cambridge University Press, 2014.

196 Peter Senge, 'The Dance of Change: The challenges to sustaining momentum in a learning organization' (The Fifth Discipline), Crown Business, 1999.

197 The late US cultural anthropologist Margaret Mead quoted by Geoffrey M. Bellman and Kathleen D. Ryan in 'Extraordinary Groups: How Ordinary Teams Achieve Amazing Results', John Wiley & Sons, 2009.

198 Margaret J. Wheatley, 'Turning to One Another: Simple Conversations to Restore Hope to the Future', Berrett-Koehler Publishers, 2009.

199 Gordon Curphy & Robert Hogan, 'The Rocket Model: Practical Advice for Building High Performing Teams,' Hogan Press, 2012.

200 Lewis Hamilton website: http://www.lewishamilton.com/

201 Peter M. Senge, 'The Fifth Discipline: The Art and Practice of The Learning Organization,' Doubleday; Revised and Updated edition, 2006.

202 J.-C. Spender & Bruce A. Strong, 'Strategic Conversations: Creating and Directing the Entrepreneurial Workforce,' Cambridge University Press, 2014.

203 Victor Frankl quote from BrainyQuote. Link: http://www.brainyquote.com/quotes/quotes/v/viktorefr160380.html

204 Christian Horner, Red Bull Team Principal quoted in 'Monaco Grand Prix: 'Screwed' Daniel Ricciardo lets rip at Red Bull over crucial pit stop delay', by Daniel Johnson, Daily Telegraph, 29th May 2016.

205 J. P. Kotter, 'A Sense of Urgency,' Harvard Business Press, 2008.

206 J. P. Kotter, 'A Sense of Urgency,' Harvard Business Press, 2008.

207 J. P. Kotter, 'A Sense of Urgency,' Harvard Business Press, 2008.

208 Scott Keller & Colin Price, 'Beyond Performance: How Great Organizations Build Ultimate Competitive Advantage', Wiley 2011.

209 Business executive quoted in 'The Five Dysfunctions of a Team' by Patrick Lencioni, Pfeiffer, 2012.

210 Larry Bossidy, Charles Burck & Ram Charan 'Execution (The Discipline of Getting Things Done),'Crown Pub. , 2009.

211 J. P. Kotter, 'A Sense of Urgency,' Harvard Business Press, 2008.

212 Neil Roberts, 'Think Fast: The Racer's Why-To Guide to Winning,' CreateSpace , 2010.

213 Garry Hammel, Foreward to 'Beyond Performance: How Great Organizations Build Ultimate Competitive Advantage', Scott Keller & Colin Price, Wiley 2011.

214 J.-C. Spender & Bruce A. Strong, 'Strategic Conversations: Creating and Directing the Entrepreneurial Workforce,' Cambridge University Press, 2014.

215 Margaret J. Wheatley, 'Turning to One Another: Simple Conversations to Restore Hope to the Future', Berrett-Koehler Publishers, 2009.

216 Juanita Brown, David Isaacs, et al., 'The World Café: Shaping Our Futures Through Conversations That Matter', Berrett-Koehler Publishers, 2005.

217 John R. Stoker, 'Overcoming Fake Talk: How to Hold REAL Conversations that Create Respect, Build Relationships, and Get Results' McGrath Professional, 2013.

218 Scott Keller & Colin Price, 'Beyond Performance: How Great Organizations Build Ultimate Competitive Advantage', Wiley 2011.

219 Robert Kegan & Lisa Laskow Lahey, 'How the Way We Talk Can Change the Way We Work', Jossey-Bass, 2007.

220 Kevin Allen, 'The Hidden Agenda: A Proven Way to Win Business and Create a Following', Bibliomotion, April 17, 2012.

221 Business executive quoted in 'The Five Dysfunctions of a Team' by Patrick Lencioni, Pfeiffer, 2012.

222 Juanita Brown, David Isaacs, et al., 'The World Café: Shaping Our Futures Through Conversations That Matter', Berrett-Koehler Publishers, 2005.

223 Action Learning is perhaps one of the best kept secrets in the business world. Yet it has its origins in the 1940's. Action Learning does 'what it says on the tin'. It is about learning by taking action.   But it is as much about change as it is about learning. It's key components are collaboration, creativity, empowerment, teamwork and personal development. To find out more about Action learning:
- Michael J. Marquardt, 'Optimizing the Power of Action Learning: Real-Time Strategies for Developing Leaders, Building Teams and Transforming Organizations', Nicholas Brealey America, 2nd Ed. 2013.
- Mike Pedler & Christine Abbott, 'Facilitating Action Learning: A Practitioner's Guide', Open University Press, 2013.

224 Rowan Gibson, 'The Four Lenses of Innovation: A Power Tool for Creative Thinking,' April 2015.

225 John Whitmore, 'Coaching for Performance: GROWing Human Potential and Purpose: The Principles and Practice of Coaching and Leadership', Nicholas Brealey Publishing; 4th Ed., 2010.

226 Ian Day & John Blakey, 'Challenging Coaching: Going beyond traditional coaching to face the FACTS', Nicholas Brealey Publishing; Reprint edition 2012).

227 'What Successful Transformations Share', McKinsey Quarterly survey, January 2010 quoted in 'Beyond Performance: How Great Organizations Build Ultimate Competitive Advantage', Scott Keller & Colin Price, Wiley 2011.

228 Patrick M. Lencioni, 'The Advantage: Why Organizational Health Trumps Everything Else In Business,' Jossey-Bass, 2012.

229 Scott Keller & Colin Price, 'Beyond Performance: How Great Organizations Build Ultimate Competitive Advantage', Wiley 2011.

230 Patrick M. Lencioni, 'The Advantage: Why Organizational Health Trumps Everything Else In Business,' Jossey-Bass, 2012.

231 Scott Keller & Colin Price, 'Beyond Performance: How Great Organizations Build Ultimate Competitive Advantage', Wiley 2011.

232 James Surowiecki, 'The Wisdom Of Crowds', Anchor, 2005.

233 Peter M. Senge, 'The Fifth Discipline: The Art and Practice of The Learning Organization,' Doubleday; Revised and Updated edition, 2006.

234 John Tiefel, "Chaos By Design: An Interview with the CEO of Zain," Voices on Transformation 3, McKinsey & Company, 2009 quoted in 'Beyond Performance: How Great Organizations Build Ultimate Competitive Advantage', Scott Keller & Colin Price, Wiley 2011.

235 Robert Kegan & Lisa Laskow Lahey, 'How the Way We Talk Can Change the Way We Work', Jossey-Bass, 2007.

236 Rita Gunther McGrath, 'The End of Competitive Advantage: How to Keep Your Strategy Moving as Fast as Your Business', 2013.

237 Gallagher, M., 'The Business of Winning: Strategic Success from the Formula One™ Track to the Boardroom,' Kogan Page, 2014.

238 Margaret Heffernan, 'A Bigger Prize: When No One Wins Unless Everyone Wins', Simon & Schuster UK, 2014.

239 Nancy Kline, 'Time to Think: Listening to Ignite the Human Mind', Cassell Illustrated, 1999.

240 W. Timothy Gallwey, 'The Inner Game of Work: Focus, Learning, Pleasure, and Mobility in the Workplace', Random House, 2001

241 William Isaacs, 'Dialog and the Art of Thinking Together: A Pioneering Approach to Communicating in Business and in Life', Bantam Doubleday Dell Publishing Group, 1999.

242 Kees van der Heijden, 'Scenarios, The Art of Strategic Conversation', Wiley, 2005.

243 John R. Stoker, 'Overcoming Fake Talk: How to Hold REAL Conversations that Create Respect, Build Relationships, and Get Results' McGrath Professional, 2013.

244 John R. Stoker, 'Overcoming Fake Talk: How to Hold REAL Conversations that Create Respect, Build Relationships, and Get Results' McGrath Professional, 2013.

245 Peter Senge, 'The Dance of Change: The challenges to sustaining momentum in a learning organization', Crown Business, 1999.

246 Dr Catherine Bailey, 'Executive Teams: Tackling tough issues', Cranfield School of Management Video: https://www.youtube.com/watch?v=7e_sb3GXUL4

247 Peter M. Senge, 'The Fifth Discipline: The Art and Practice of The Learning Organization,' Doubleday; Revised and Updated edition, 2006.

248 Janna Raye Petaluma 'FRACTAL ORGANIZATION THEORY', Proceedings of the 56th Annual Meeting of the ISSS – 2012.

249 Ken Catchpol, Marc De Kevakm et al, 'Patient handover from surgery to intensive care: using Formula 1™ pit-stop and aviation models to improve safety and quality,' Pediatric Anesthesia Volume 17, Issue 5, May 2007.

250 Gary Hamel "The Search for Strategy"
quoted in 'The World Café: Shaping Our Futures Through Conversations That Matter' by Juanita Brown, et al., Berrett-Koehler Publishers, 2005

251 Research by Angus Hildreth and Cameron Anderson at UC Berkeley Haas School of Business as featured on NPR Morning Edition, March 11 2016 by Shankar Vedantam; 'Why A Group's Power Dynamics Interferes With Collaboration', Link: http://www.npr.org/2016/03/11/470040275/why-a-groups-power-dynamics-interferes-with-collaboration

252 Yves Morieux and Peter Tollman, in their book '6 Simple Rules', Harvard Business Review Press, 2014.

253 IBM Design Thinking Principles – 'a framework for teaming and action'. Link: http://www.ibm.com/design/thinking/

254 Margaret Heffernan, 'Willful Blindness: Why We Ignore the Obvious', Simon & Schuster UK, 2012.

255 J.-C. Spender & Bruce A. Strong, 'Strategic Conversations: Creating and Directing the Entrepreneurial Workforce,' Cambridge University Press, 2014.

256 Peter M. Senge, 'The Fifth Discipline: The Art and Practice of The Learning Organization,' Doubleday; Revised and Updated edition, 2006.

257 Dan Ariely, 'Predictably Irrational: The Hidden Forces that Shape Our Decisions', HarperCollins, 2009.

258 Boris Groysberg, 'Chasing Stars: The Myth of Talent and the Portability of Performance', Princeton University Press, 2012.

259 Nancy Kline, 'Time to Think: Listening to Ignite the Human Mind', Cassell Illustrated, 1999.

260 William Isaacs, 'Dialog and the Art of Thinking Together: A Pioneering Approach to Communicating in Business and in Life', Bantam Doubleday Dell Publishing Group, 1999.

261 Nancy Kline, 'Time to Think: Listening to Ignite the Human Mind', Cassell Illustrated, 1999.

262 J.-C. Spender & Bruce A. Strong, 'Strategic Conversations: Creating and Directing the Entrepreneurial Workforce,' Cambridge University Press, 2014.

263 Patrick Thean, 'Rhythm: How to Achieve Breakthrough Execution and Accelerate Growth,' Greenleaf Book Group, 2014.

264 Gillian Tett, 'The Silo Effect: Why putting everything in its place isn't such a bright idea', Little Brown, 2015.

265 Juanita Brown, David Isaacs, et al., 'The World Café: Shaping Our Futures Through Conversations That Matter', Berrett-Koehler Publishers, 2005.

266 Tim Jones, Dave McCormick & Caroline Dewing, 'Growth Champions: The Battle for Sustained Innovation Leadership (Growth Agenda)', John Wiley & Sons, Mar 2012.

267 Sean Ellis & Morgan Brown, 'Startup Growth Engines: Case Studies of

How Today's Most Successful Startups Unlock Extraordinary Growth', Ellis & Brown Publishing 2014.

268 Peter M. Senge, 'The Fifth Discipline: The Art and Practice of The Learning Organization,' Doubleday; Revised and Updated edition, 2006.

269 IBM Design Thinking Principles – 'a framework for teaming and action'. Link: http://www.ibm.com/design/thinking/

270 William Isaacs, 'Dialog and the Art of Thinking Together: A Pioneering Approach to Communicating in Business and in Life', Bantam Doubleday Dell Publishing Group, 1999.

271 Alex "Sandy" Pentland, 'The New Science of Building Great Teams', HBR, Apr. 2012. This research in a call centre environment suggests that patterns of communication among teams (in particular levels of energy, exploration and engagement) account for as much as 50% of the performance gap between the worst and the best. Link: https://hbr.org/2012/04/the-new-science-of-building-great-teams/ar/1

272 John R. Stoker, 'Overcoming Fake Talk: How to Hold REAL Conversations that Create Respect, Build Relationships, and Get Results' McGrath Professional, 2013.

273 http://www.f1-grandprix.com/?page_id=28278

274 Mario Andretti retired Italian-American world champion racing driver quoted on BrainyQuote: http://www.brainyquote.com/quotes/quotes/m/marioandre636602.html

275 Gallagher, M., 'The Business of Winning: Strategic Success from the Formula One™ Track to the Boardroom,' Kogan Page, 2014.

276 Mark Jenkins, Ken Pasternak, Richard West, 'Performance at the Limit: Business Lessons from Formula 1® Motor Racing', Cambridge University Press; 3 edition (2 Jun. 2016).

277 Lewis Hamilton quoted after the 2014 US Grand Prix - his 10th win of the season on formulaspy.com. Link: http://formulaspy.com/news/formula-1-news/2014-united-states-gp-driver-quotes-7503

278 Larry Dixon is a celebrated American professional drag racer in the National Hot Rod Assocation. Quote from Brainy Quote. Link:http://www.brainyquote.com/quotes/quotes/l/larrydixon277478.html

279 Danica Patrick is the most successful woman in the history of American open-wheel racing (https://en.wikipedia.org/wiki/Danica_Patrick). Quote from: http://www.brainyquote.com/quotes/authors/d/danica_patrick_2.html

280 Michael Schumacher interviewed by Jonathan Noble in 2002 related in Daly, D. 'Race to Win: How to Become a Complete Champion Driver,' Motorbooks, 2008.

Your Notes & Doodles

Lightning Source UK Ltd.
Milton Keynes UK
UKHW020342230119
336046UK00005B/133/P